Garvey's Children

The Legacy of Marcus Garvey

Tony Sewell

CARIBBEAN

First published 1987 by Voice Communications Ltd
This edition published 1990 by
MACMILLAN EDUCATION LTD
London and Basingstoke
Companies and representatives throughout the world

ISBN 0–333–49124–6

11	10	9	8	7	6	5	4	3	2
07	06	05	04	03	02	01	00	99	98

This book is printed on paper suitable for recycling and
made from fully managed and sustained forest sources.

Printed in Hong Kong

A catalogue record for this book is available from the
British Library.

Photography:
Derek Bishton   Mervyn Weir
Race Today   Institute of Jamaica
Lennox Smiley   Jamaica Information Service
Sharon Wallace
Shar Reichenstein

CONTENTS

To My Mother

"The Coloured race is greatly in need of a Moses — one that is not hand-picked or controlled by the blandishments of official environment — a man of the people and designated by the people." Washington Bee 1918

"If I were to choose six people, who had the greatest influence on the twentieth century, then Marcus Garvey would be one and he wouldn't be sixth."
C.L.R. James

"The small axe will chop the big tree." Bob Marley

Foreword

Marcus Mosiah Garvey deserves to be the icon he has become to millions of people of African ancestry throughout the world because of the seminal contribution he made to the liberation struggles of blacks both on the African Continent and in the Diaspora. What he has left behind is a legacy of philosophy and opinions in the fight against the continuing humiliation of Black African civilisation and its variants in the Americas (including the Caribbean) and among migrant blacks in Europe. He remains a source of energy for the efforts of those who love freedom and abhor the bigotry of racial discrimination — an eloquent tribute to his deep insights into the human condition. The vision he had for a world that needed redemption from racism and its vilest consequences, is as relevant today as it was in the 1920s.

He remains controversial, therefore. On the one hand, there is the fact of a popular grasp of the greatness and value of the man to black civilisation and indeed to all mankind struggling with the dilemmas of cultural and racial identity, and the psychological confusion about the dynamics of power, and how it eludes the marginalised mass which happens to be black. On the other hand, there is the doubt of a people who are yet to grasp the full measure of their real place in the wider world. For that place is determined not only by the historical relations of dependency of colonial periphery on metropolitan centre, or of a technologically advanced and economically prosperous north lording it over an underdeveloped south. It rests as well on the entrenched notions of a natural superiority claimed by certain civilisations over others in terms of the capacities to shape their own destinies by invention and creative thinking in ways that advance human development.

So whether it is in the area of language or religion, of family structures or artistic manifestations, of political systems or economic processes of production, distribution and exchange, Africa's offspring have long been deemed incapable of advancing humanity unless with the civilising assistance of Europe. It is this fundamental canon of Western thought and ideology (whether of right, centre, or left) that Garvey spent a lifetime challenging. The instincts and deep subconscious of the black populations scattered all over the Western world and particularly in the Americas, give them a full grasp of the import of this concern.

Every means, then, has had to be found not simply to have black people re-possess themselves and their space in the mainstream of human existence, but to dig out the cancerous bodies of ideas that would seek to perpetuate the subjugated condition of Africa's children in the Americas and of Africans on the Continent itself.

It is the totality of Garvey's assault upon this madness that gives him a permanent place in the gallery of thinkers on the universal and perennial themes of freedom and liberation, social justice, and what for the twentieth century has been the legacy of imperial expansion namely, racial prejudice and the attendant cruelties against humanity.

Anti-imperialism has become, and still is, a function of ethnic and cultural assertion. The fact that the colonised were not Caucasian played no small part in maintaining the imperial raj throughout the globe — whether in India, South East Asia, Africa or the Caribbean. It is no accident that the name of Marcus Garvey was anathema to all the imperial powers of Europe in the Twenties and Thirties. And the banning of his *Negro World* bore testimony to the fear he struck in the hearts of those who were not yet prepared to preside over the liquidation of their control over the wealth, minds and spirit of subject peoples among so-called "lesser races". Colonial powers in Garvey's time thought that colonialism would last for centuries more, if not forever. Garvey did not!

It is in his determined, disciplined, unrelenting focus on the cause at hand and his deep insights into the condition of millions of humanity, which marked Garvey off from many others who at the time thought of Africa and her children overseas. And her children overseas together formed the extension of an entire civilisation which in Garvey's own words was his primary area of concern. Universal ideas, he insisted, knew no territorial boundaries: they could not in any case, since the "nation" of black people was anywhere they were to be found. And his travels to Central America, the Caribbean and all over the United States where most of the blacks outside of Africa then lived were a mark of his global view of what his remit really was.

He established a track record for the Universal Negro Improvement Association in championing the cause of West Indian migrant workers usually in hostile host settings. Central to all this was the need for those black workers or black citizens of these republics to put their energies towards helping to build not only a great African nation on the continent, but a black civilisation that could claim its rightful place in the human family.

That rightful place would only come, he felt, if the black man saw to the honing of his intellectual, political and scientific power, Garvey insisted. What an excellent reminder in these times when many political leaders in the black world continue to ignore the need to build their societies on the basis of creative intellect and imagination!

Garvey, though no revolutionary of the cataclysmic mould, would not rule out armed conflict in the pursuit of freedom if it came to that, as his sympathies for the Irish rebellion clearly indicate. His views on apartheid-bound South Africa is here quite predictable.

But at heart he was a builder, always accentuating the positive in terms of self-reliance, self-development, the release of labour from the strictures of capital, the shaping of a society rooted in economic viability, coordinated social action, cultural certitude and intellectual muscle. No Jamaican founding father has come better than that in the conseptualisation of a new Jamaica — the one that is yet to be totally liberated from the entrapment in dependency on metropolitan (and for Garvey this meant white and it still means white) economics, politics, artistic achievement and ideas about all these things.

To make the kind of symbolic assaults as he did on the hallowed power structures of the white ruling world was considered impertinent and of course made a target of derision among his detractors. He is indeed photographed in scholar's robes, in emperor's garb, and in the habit of a gentleman of quality. Like a civilisation in exile, he organised his movement into one with a virtual government, with mechanisms for economic and industrial action (Black Star Line et al), with foreign delegations (missions to Liberia etc), with a communications system (newspapers and pamphlets), with a hierarchy of titled citizens, with auxiliary institutions of growth (youth groups, Black Cross nurses) and so on, following the established institutional frameworks of the dominant and oppressive society.

Some of his detractors for this reason suggest that he was himself trapped in the white world's agenda. But Garvey never made any secret of his belief that the ancient civilisations of Africa in the Nile were the source of energy for all mankind. The white world therefore had no monopoly on social organisation, intellectual ordering of experience, cultural products of the imagination, or on the administration of power.

By the time he was forced to return to Jamaica, he could present a manifesto on behalf of his Peoples Political Party which he launched in 1929. The 14 plank platform is very much the basis of what became the core of the mission statement of the self-government movement formally launched nine years later and which event, pursued with vigour and Westminster logic, brought his native Jamaica to Independence in 1962.

But Garvey's mission is yet to be accomplished. By going for fundamental change Garvey has told succeeding generations that he was well aware of the possibility of liberation eluding the blacks despite political independence. Nor did he see race-pride in purely epidermal dimensions. He understood the value of work and the responsibility of any race of people to exercise their intellect and imagination in their own interest. He also understood the viability of a black civilisation rooted in the facts of a history that preceded even that of the people who would dare to keep down Africans in some form of modern-day mental slavery. He felt the emancipation from that state of existence was critical to the development of people everywhere.

That mental slavery is still evident among blacks. That is why one of his heirs in the person of the late Bob Marley enjoined blacks to do the job themselves. All indeed is not lost; for the man's message persists among such other legatees as Burning Spear, Jimmy Cliff, Peter Tosh and the dub poet Mutabaruka — poets of utterance all and, like Marcus Garvey, their mentor, intellectuals of a special stamp who will in future provide the grist for the doctoral mills in universities all over the world.

Precisely because Garvey has earned and maintained popular recognition he is deserving of serious and deep study. For he is not the "utopian, buffoon, unprincipled character, thief. . .or con-man" that detractors love to present him as, though such has been "the lot of those who have stood up for fundamental change" as Rupert Lewis, the Garvey scholar, says.

There is indeed much work yet to be done by "political scientists, cultural analysts, historians, journalists, theologians, philosophers. . . ." on this twentieth century prophet, priest and "king".

Professor Rex Nettleford
University of the West Indies

RESURRECTION IN LONDON

SON: Say, father, why is it I am born black and placed at such a disadvantage among other boys in the world?

FATHER: My son, to be born black is no disgrace nor misfortune. It is an honour. Nature never intended humanity to be of one colour or complexion, and so there are different races or types of people in the world. There are standard types and the Negro is one of them. In the history of the world the Negro has had a glorious career. In the centuries past he was greater than any other race, but, unfortunately, today he occupies a position not as favourable as that of his fathers.

SON: But father, everywhere I go I hear and see people speaking and acting disrespectfully toward the Negro.

FATHER: That is true, my son, but that doesn't mean that to be black is to be really inferior. It is only because the economic condition of the blackman is so low to-day why other peoples do not entirely respect him. It is, therefore, due to his own neglect, and not to any cause of natural inferiority.

SON: Does that mean, father, that if the Negro wants he can be as honourable, progressive and dignified as any other race?

FATHER: Yes, my son, that's it. In this world we are what we make ourselves. The Negro is just an individual like anyone else, and, individually, he can make himself what he wants to be. In the same respect the individuals of a race becoming a congregation of a whole can make themselves what they want to be.

A Dialogue: What's the difference? by Marcus Garvey.

"No one remembers old Marcus Garvey, no one remembers old Marcus Garvey." I turned up the cassette player as the sounds of Burning Spear began to shake my rather rust eaten Datsun. I had driven through this part of the Harrow Road on many occasions, yet as I approached St Mary's Catholic cemetery, I began to feel that I was making a pilgrimage. The road-sweeper's instructions were correct: you keep driving along the Harrow Road, just before you turn into Ladbroke Grove, you'll see a flower shop on the right and St Mary's will be opposite on the left.

I walked quickly through the cemetery. Statues of Jesus and Mary stood above graves that seemed to be populated with Irish and Italians. An old gardener feebly hacked at the nearby bushes; I asked him if he could remember the summer of 1940: "Yes, it was sheer hell son, you see that launderette across the road, well that used to be the butchers. Each morning there'd be a long queue; it would stretch for a good 100 yards; just to get chicken wings and sausage meat. It was the war; all of Europe was blowing itself to bits."

The year 1940 was one of the bleakest in memory; children on the coast at Southampton could hear German shells in France. The French had been invaded and there was a call on the radio for a day of prayer. In London, the army could commandeer your house or the war ministry could force you to house evacuees. The only bright spark for London was that West Ham had beaten Blackburn Rovers at Wembley (1–0) to take the war-time Cup Final. The rest was misery, all lights had to be out at 9pm and not be turned on until 4.48am while food was by ration book only. Garvey probably read the case of poor Mrs Dorothy Hooper of Lillie Road, Fulham, who was fined 20 shillings for not screening a light, but whose house was hit the next week by a stray bomb even though she was in total darkness.

Previous page:
St Mary's Cemetery, West London

As I entered the cosy chapel I thought of the coffin of Marcus Garvey, resting

on the altar; no flags, no honours and few tears — yet this was the funeral of a hero, the man who had a world-wide following of over 11 million people. I was shown the records of his funeral which took place on June 14th, 1940, four days after his death. Garvey lived and died at 53 Talgarth Road, West Kensington, his last place of abode since his exile from Jamaica in 1935. He was only 52.

Father Clark conducted the funeral service of Marcus Garvey, who received all the blessings of a Catholic burial. The world went on without giving honour to one of the great men of the twentieth century. Garvey was not even mentioned in his local West Kensington newspaper.

Like a latter day Christ, Garvey was not actually buried but the body was put into the musty catacomb in the huge basement below the chapel. I walked around this expanse of death; there were many unnamed coffins stacked like vintage wines. Garvey's body was to stay there until October 6th, 1964 when the Jamaican Government requested that the body be returned to Jamaica, where Garvey would be buried and duly honoured as Jamaica's first national hero.

Another person who made the trip to this chapel some years after his death, was Garvey's first wife, Amy Ashwood, whom Garvey divorced after he accused her of seeing other men. Amy never stopped loving him and it was left to her to mourn the death of her beloved. His second wife, Amy Jacques Garvey, was not at the funeral; her youngest son Marcus Jr, was ill, and after coming to England with Garvey in 1935, she had returned, in 1938, to the healthier climes of Jamaica. This, however, seemed to be a kind of separation because Garvey later wrote: "I shall not be returning to Jamaica and ... in case anything happens to me I want you to know that I have opened a Post Office account at the West Kensington North End Road W14, Post Office in your name."

It was back in February 1938 that Garvey rented a house at Talgarth Road. Amy Jacques recalls the time in her memoirs: "Colored children . . . . . were rarely seen in England at this time, so Garvey enjoyed taking the boys out, as they attracted attention. Junior went more often, as they could discuss cinema shows. He was intrigued by English remarks such as: 'Aren't they lovely? . . . . . such large black eyes! What beautiful white teeth! They speak English, too. Can I touch him for

Amy Jacques Garvey with sons Julius (right) and Marcus Jr (left). They led the funeral procession in Jamaica, when Garvey's body was returned to his homeland.

luck?' Junior became so accustomed to being admired, that one morning when I was taking them to school, he stopped suddenly, and said, 'Mom, is anything wrong with me?' I looked him over, and assured him that he was just right for parade inspection. 'Oh,' said he, 'that's not for today. No girls admire me this morning'.''

Outside the cemetery, an advert for Lucozade showed athlete Daley Thompson in pursuit of another victory. It made me reflect on the positive thinking of Garvey, who preached the philosophy of 'success' — a philosophy for black people to believe in their ability and right to a place in the world. I remembered reading one of his last speeches, where he drew parables from his own life for the instruction of his followers: ''I am trying . . . . to make everyone a Marcus Garvey personified. I came from a surrounding not better than many of you, but my mind lifted me out of my surroundings.'' He went on: ''I was born in the country town of St Ann's Bay . . . And in my tender years I went to my father's books and I gathered inspiration, and what inspiration I gathered, changed my outlook from the ambition of wanting to be a wharf-man or cow-boy, and made me look forward to being a personality in the world. Nobody helped me toward that objective except my own mind and God's good will, and during 44 years of struggle I brought myself from the possibility of a cow-boy to a man who is known in many continents.''

Garvey in 1935 was a man in exile, living with his white friends in London after he had found it impossible to organise his movement for 'Negro Improvement' from Jamaica. He wanted to retrench in London and develop his movement once again. In 1935 he wrote in his newspaper, *The Blackman*, some reasons why he had chosen voluntary exile from Jamaica: "There are a few good men in Jamaica, the national disposition seems to be that of enthroned selfishness. Further, there is no love of countryman, and so anyone going to Jamaica will see that the most prosperous people on the island are aliens, particularly Asiatics. Their control of the island is made easy because the people who are natives hate themselves to such a terrible extent that they easily open up the way for the outsider to get the advantage." He goes on: "The Jamaicans hate themselves because they constitute a mixed population.The people in Jamaica worship colour, that is the colour of the skin. They think it is the greatest and best thing in life, hence people who are even related by blood, if they are not of the same complexion, hate and despise each other."

London, even though it was on the brink of war, provided Garvey with a sense of peace compared to the colour madness and hounding he received in Jamaica. Garvey always maintained that his quarrel was never with the black majority in Jamaica but with the brown elite who should have known better. One black celebrity who spent time in London while Garvey was there, was actor/singer Paul Robeson. When Robeson was leaving for Hollywood, Garvey launched a vicious attack on some of the roles that the actor was prepared to play. He says: "We admire Paul Robeson as an artist, but as a representative of the race he is a poor specimen, in that he always allows himself to be featured in those plays that do more harm than good to his race. He has gone there to make another slanderous picture against the Negro. He is to be one of the stars in the new picture, 'Stevedore'. This is a propaganda play engineered for the purpose of emphasizing Negro inferiority and white superiority . . . ''

There were few other black people in London during the 1930s but Garvey was extremely popular with his many white friends and he was offered a liberal tolerance that he badly needed. His private secretary, Daisy White, recalls how he was missed when, through illness, he had to give up speaking at Hyde Park "I am not surprised on my return here (Jamaica) to hear that some people did not believe that he was sick for so many months as he was seen driving in Hyde Park. Well, we did take him driving in Hyde Park during his illness when he felt brighter, and many of his former audiences in the Park greeted him not knowing he was unable to walk. He was very sensitive about this, as he never wanted people to know that he was crippled in one side.''

During the early part of Marcus Garvey's London years, the Italians had invaded Ethiopia and the war had really smashed Garvey's dream of building a United States of Africa. It also saw the demise of his once-great organisation to virtually nothing. When his death came, however, many of his predictions were being realised: Jamaica was experiencing one of the biggest workers' revolts in its history, European powers were in a massive struggle which resulted in the Second World War, while uprisings were reported daily in all the colonies. The African freedom struggle, which would become a revolution 20 years later, was without doubt stimulated by the Garvey legacy.

In January 1940 he suffered a first stroke which left him paralysed but he improved with the help of a specialist. Later that year, in May, a black reporter in England maliciously gave out the news that Garvey had died in poverty in London. Many letters of condolence poured into his office following publication of the report in the Jamaican newspaper, the *Gleaner*. Seeing these letters, the stress became too much and Garvey fell back on his pillow, dead.

What is sad about the *Gleaner* article is that no attempt was made to check the authenticity of the report which, on May 18th, announced that "Garvey is dead" on the front page. The nature of the article, in any case no way befitted that of a national hero: there are no condolences from any leading figures and the obituary was taken from *Who's Who*. The black journalist who was the source of the story was George Padmore, a key figure in the African liberation struggles. At a meeting in Hyde Park on August 8th, 1937, Garvey had been heckled by Padmore and C.L.R. James, who called upon him to declare his stand on the working class

Paul Robeson plays Othello, a role that Garvey would have approved.

Today
SEE PAGE 28

The Daily Gleaner.

ESTABLISHED 1834 ESTABLISHED 1834

MYERS'S
Planters' Punch
FINE OLD JAMAICA RUM
OVER 8 YEARS IN WOOD
FRED L. MYERS & SON — (FOUNDED 1879)
"The Sugar Wharf" Kingston

THIRTY-TWO PAGES | Vol. CVI. No. 116. | KINGSTON, JAMAICA, SATURDAY, MAY 18, 1940. | Price: PENNY HALF-PENNY | THIRTY-TWO PAGES

NAZIS PRESS WAY INTO BRUSSELS IN THRUST TOWARD ANTWERP

Sweeping Drive Brings Germans Within Seventy Miles Of Paris

FRENCH HALT PUSH AS GAMELIN CALLS ON MEN FOR SUPREME SACRIFICE

LONDON, May 17.—Germany's motorized blitzkrieg columns plunged across eastern Belgium to claim Brussels and Louvain tonight and to threaten Belgium's chief channel port of Antwerp. The lightning thrust in Belgium followed swiftly upon the heels of the German drive into northeastern France which brought the head of the Nazi column within threatening distance of Rheims and within seventy miles of Paris, itself.

In the face of the battering German attack, the Allied Commander in Chief, General Gamelin, called upon French troops to die in their positions before they yielded an inch of French soil.

French military sources said that the German forces in France were attacking with violence at only one point. That was at the foot of the sixty-mile pocket which the Germans drove into the northern extension of the Maginot line, northwest of Rethel.

Paris and London made no comment on the German claims that the Allied defences had collapsed on the Dyle line in Belgium opening the way for a march on Brussels and a thrust toward Antwerp.

British forces were supporting the Belgian line at Louvain which the Germans said had been taken when the Anglo-Belgian line fell back. The retreat of the Belgians from the Dyle line before Louvain was indicated in the nightly Belgian communique, which said: "Our troops methodically carried out the movements provided for in our plan of operations."

The communique was issued from the Belgian seaside resort of Ostend which became the temporary Belgian capital to-day when the Government abandoned Brussels. The Government moved its headquarters after the Germans had threatened to bomb Brussels as a fortified city.

GERMANS CLAIM CAPTURE OF FRENCH FORCE

The Germans claimed the capture of two French Generals with their entire staffs and a force of 12,000 men, approximately a division. Huge quantities of war material were claimed to have been taken with the capture of the French troops. The Germans also claimed to have annihilated a Brigade of Algerian troops and a regiment of Norman troops in their drive into France.

The French High Command reported tonight that a great battle was in progress north of St. Quentin, inside the French-Belgian frontier.

Heavy German tank attacks were reported by the French High Command to be concentrated along a line extending from Avesnes, twenty miles southwards to Vervins.

The object of this attack apparently is to push the left wing of the Allied forces back toward the sea, while splitting the British and French forces and cutting off the Allied and Belgian forces in Belgium.

Said the French war communique: "The German attack developed today on a massive scale not only in Belgium, but in the region of Avesnes and Vervines. The enemy engaged on the whole of this front the greater part of his heavy tank divisions. The battle assumed the characteristic of a veritable melee.

(Continued on page 17)

Garvey Dies In London

A CABLE & WIRELESS Dispatch from New York yesterday afternoon announced the death in London recently of Mr. Marcus Garvey after an illness of some months.

Marcus Garvey, who rose from a very humble position in life to be one of the greatest leaders of his race—in fact one of the most colourful figures of any race—in modern times, was stricken, according to reports received here, with paralysis in his London home some months ago, and from the onset it was feared that his illness would be fatal. But he fought gamely on, attended by specialists, and the latest news that reached the island a few days ago was that he was progressing. He must have had a sudden relapse, but the cable which came to hand yesterday did not state the date of his death.

The son of Marcus and Sarah Garvey, the man who was to become in early years of mature life a world figure was born at St. Ann's Bay in August 1887. He was educated at elementary schools and by private tuition, and started out in life as a printer in 1903, holding employment at the "Gleaner" and the Government Printing Office until 1909.

SELF-MADE MAN

During this period he was preparing himself for his life's work. Through his mind flowed plans for the improvement and uplift of the coloured people and these he frequently discussed with friends and colleagues, at street corners and meetings. He branched out into journalistic work, and realising the limitation of his field in Jamaica, left the island in 1909, travelling and lecturing in South and Central America. Soon the name of Marcus Garvey began to be bruited about and he returned to Jamaica in 1911 with a fast-rising reputation of orator and student of political economy directed to the uplifting of his race. His next trip abroad took him to England where he obtained a position on the "African Times" and "Orient Review." This was in 1913.

Garvey's plans were now matured and he was headed to launch a movement that was to bring him into world prominence. Returning to Jamaica, he organised the Universal Negro Improvement Association in 1914. Speedily, hundreds came under his banner but once again the land of his birth was too small for the scheme he had envisioned. His eyes turned to the United States where he felt he could find the fullest scope for his activities, and to America he went shortly after.

DYNAMIC SPEAKER

1917 and 1918 found him travelling through the United States propounding his thesis for negro improvement. Thousands flocked to hear him wherever he went, and in the latter year he organised the New York branch of the U.N.I.A. Soon his following ran into hundreds of thousands; some claimed millions, and Marcus Garvey, the Jamaican, was acclaimed the Moses of the coloured race.

He established and edited a newspaper called "The Negro World" which was printed from 1918 to 1923. He organised the Black Star Line Steamship Coy., to trade between American and West Indian ports, but the venture was not a success, in fact, the one ocean-going vessel owned by the Line only made one trip.

In 1919 Garvey was elected President General of the U.N.I.A. and his oratory swayed vast crowds, at the headquarters, Liberty Hall, Harlem, New York. In 1920 he organised the Negro Factors Corporation and African Communities League.

Garvey was now taking active interest in American politics and it was freely stated at the time that he could command three to four million negro votes. He raised powerful political enemies and a

(Continued on page 17)

Belgian Govt. At Ostend

OSTEND, May 17.—The Belgian Government has been established at this important Belgian post since yesterday. It can now be revealed that the Government left Brussels in complete secrecy in agreement with the Belgian High Command. At one point which cannot be revealed German planes bombed several automobiles belonging to the administrative personnel just before the cars carrying Government members passed. A number of diplomatic missions, notably Argentine, Peru and Yugoslavia also moved to Ostend. The Spanish Ambassador is in the vicinity. The Papal Nuncio, the United States embassy and the Italian Ambassador remained at Brussels.

The Brussels radio broadcast an exhortation to the little country's army to make a stand for King Leopold in 1940 like that their fathers made for King Albert in 1914. The announcer urged all Belgians to remember the slogan of King Albert: "A people that defends itself cannot die."—Wireless and Canadian Press by Cable and Wireless Ltd.

R. A. F. Attack Oil Tanks At Bergen

Sensational Stories Tell Of German Casualties In Norwegian Campaign

LONDON, May 16.—The Air Ministry announced a successful Royal Air Force attack on oil storage tanks at Berger, Norway, held by German forces. Other R. A. F. airraids were made against Nazi airplane and supply bases at Slorgaaspynt, Strudsaven and Attknarven.

The Foreign Minister, Viscount Halifax, told Norwegian officials to-day that the Allies would continue their fight in Norway despite the spread of the war to other fronts. Lord Halifax said the first objective in Norway would be the capture of the Northern port of Narvik as a base of operations for Norwegian troops. Said the Foreign Minister: "When Narvik is captured we shall confer with Norwegian officials to see what way the situation can be developed best to our mutual advantage."

The Swedish radio heard in London to-day said that Norwegian and Allied troops have withdrawn from some position around Narvik.—Wireless.

GERMAN CASUALTIES.

STOCKHOLM, May 15.—Sensational stories indicating that the

(Continued on page 17)

"Gleaner" Football Contest

ENTRIES CLOSE

TODAY

18th May

Money is not too plentiful at the present time! But the Gleaner's Missing Ball Competition gives you the wonderful chance for a 3d to win £250 (which is the first prize, or many another big cash prize).

ONLY 3D FOR EACH ENTRY

If you could use £250 then TRY to get £250. Don't just wish for it—Make a determined effort to get it! Enter our Football Competition NOW!

Remember the prizes are there to be won. It is for you to try, because you cannot hope to win unless you try! Why not do this now? You have little to lose and a LOT to win! See page 28.

How Hitler's Men Carried Out Blitzkrieg In Holland

Soldiers crossing flooded areas in rubber boats —New York Times photo

Gamelin Bids Army "Conquer Or Die"

GENERAL GAMELIN

PARIS, May 17:—The Allied Generalissimo, General Gamelin, called upon the French Army to rally itself, like it did on the Marne in 1914 and save France and Western civilization.

The order of the day issued to the French Army by General Gamelin warned that France's whole existence and that of her Allies as well is at stake in the battle now waging north of Paris where German troops broke through the Maginot defences.

Said General Gamelin: "The fate of our country and that of our Allies and the destinies of the world depend on the battle which is now in progress. British, Belgian, Polish soldiers and foreign volunteers fighting on our side, and the Royal Air Force, are taking their full task with our own. Any soldier who cannot advance should allow himself to be killed rather than abandon that part of our national soil which was confided to him. As always in the grave hours of our history the order today is 'Conquer, or die.' We must conquer."

The trumpet like words of General Gamelin sounded the cry of all France and of her Allies. It instilled new courage in the hard-pressed French forces and brought prompt successes in strong counter-attacks in the Sedan and Malmedy sectors.—Wireless.

Child Drowned While Crossing River In Spate

SPRING HILL, May 17:—(By telegraph from our Correspondent).—The infant son of Mr. Younis Taylor of this district came to his death by drowning in the Shantamee River yesterday while crossing the flooded stream with his father. The body of the child has not yet been found.

Heavy and incessant rains still continue here.

Supreme War Council Meet

Mr. Churchill In Paris

PARIS, May 17.—Supreme War Council meeting Thursday was of exceptional importance for progress of current military operations and preparation of plans future, an authorized spokesman said. Present were Mr. Churchill, M. Reynaud, M. Daladier and General Gamelin.

Mr Churchill's visit to Paris was most heartening to both countries, and the French paid warm tributes today to his dynamic personality and his firm resolution. The resolution of such men as he and General Gamelin gives heart to all of us.—Wireless and Canadian Press by Cable and Wireless Ltd.

Strategic British Withdrawal From Belgian Position

Public Asked To Keep Stout Heart And Cool Head

LONDON, May 17.—The position in Belgium known as the Dyle line, which British troops held for some days against heavy German attacks have now been abandoned and Allied Forces have withdrawn to a position which correspond better to the situation further south.

The War Office announced that British troops had withdrawn to prepared positions west of Brussels but the readjustment was carried out without interference. The public was called upon to keep a stout heart and cool heads," by an authoritative source. "Britain has faced tests like this before," the War Office declared. "There is no question of collapse or break through." The Brussels sector was where Allied and Belgian troops fought bitterly to halt the Germans east of the city and vicinity of Louvain.

Following the strategic withdrawal of the British troops are now at Dugin along the canal that runs south of Brussels.—Wireless and Canadian Press by Cable and Wireless Ltd.

LAST DAY FOR PROVERB CONTEST

This afternoon is the closing hour for our latest Jamaica Proverb Contest, with its tempting prize of £3 3/- for the correct solution. But entries bearing this afternoon's postmark received by Monday's first post will be admitted.

Today is the last day for sending in your entries.—send as many as you like, with three pence for each.

The winner or winners will be announced next Saturday.

Italy Seen In The War By Monday

PARIS, May 17.—War clouds gathered thick and fast over the Mediterranean to-day with increasing indications that Fascist Italy will enter the war on or before May 20.

The German break-through of the Maginot Line extension in the Sedan—Givet sector, and the advance of the Nazi armoured divisions toward Paris provoked Italian Cabinet leaders and Fascist spokesmen to declare openly that the hour is near when Italy will act.

Premier Mussolini appeared clearing the decks for a sudden attack upon France and upon the Suez, by land, air and naval forces, when the Nazi legions have reached the Marne. Complete secrecy was maintained by Italian military leaders but there was no denying that the Italian populace was being whipped into a war frenzy by spoken and printed imprecations against the Allies, and particularly against Britain's dominance of the Mediterranean.

The keynote of the rising crescendo of war fever was sounded by the Italian Minister of Education, Bottai, in the Critica Fascista.

THE CRUCIAL HOUR

Said the Italian Minister: "The Mediterranean is our sea. We must liberate ourselves from British control of this vital waterway. We

(Continued on page 17)

R.A.F. Attacks Harass Nazis

Eleven British Aircraft Failed To Return

LONDON, May 17.—The Air Ministry issued an announcement which showed that last night forces of medium bombers made sustained attacks on enemy transports and petrol reserves in the woods round Sedan.

The announcement said that attacks were also made on troop reserves and supply columns. As a result of these operations several fires broke out. During yesterday enemy troops in the valley of the Meuse were fiercely and successfully attacked.

Pontoon bridges were blown up, roads blocked and troops on the main road bombed and machine-gunned.

The enemy was harassed and hampered at key points and mechanised troops received heavy casualties.

The communique went on: "There has been intense activity in the B. E. F. area to-day. Bomber squadrons of the Royal Air Force made repeated and determined attacks on mechanised enemy columns. The enemy advance was protected by strong fighter formations. Nevertheless our bombers made a series of low flying attacks on enemy columns and inflicted great damage.

In support of the French army a squadron of Blenheims this morning bombed key positions twenty miles south of Louvain. In spite of great gallantry and determination by our aircraft, 11 of our aircraft failed to return.—Wireless.

THE SUNDAY GLEANER

War News And Agatha Christie's Great Detective Serial In Tomorrow's Issue

THE WAR NEWS, and the opening chapters of Agatha Christie's great detective serial, featuring the famous fiction detective Hercules Pierot, boosted last week's Sunday Gleaner to a sale of over 16,000 copies. It is certain that there will be a much larger circulation of to-morrow's issue for to-day's and to-night's war news will be of a nature that might have a tremendous bearing on the future welfare of every citizen of the British Empire. The fate of nations is in the balance and to-morrow's Sunday Gleaner will contain the last-minute reports of all the news received by wireless, radio and cables.

Then there is the second instalment of "Sad Cypress," an intriguing murder mystery of jealousy, greed and love, packed with thrills from beginning to end. You must read it in the Sunday Gleaner for it is not being run in the daily issue.

Other features cover various phases of the war with its far-flung ramifications, written by men well-qualified to deal with their subject and a character sketch of Lord Lloyd, the new head of the Colonial Office, and an article by the Rt. Hon. Hore-Belisha, former Secretary of State for war, on the changed Scandinavian situation as it affects the fortunes of England and Germany.

Then there will be the latest outstanding local events and results of the cricket matches and other sports.

In its eight pages will also be found a number of up-to-date war pictures. The price is 1d, and the Sunday Gleaner reaches into all parts of Jamaica.

Order your copy to-day.

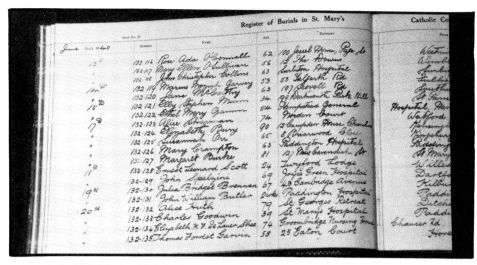

Register of Burials, which shows the entry of Marcus Garvey. It goes on to give details about the body being taken back to Jamaica in 1964.

struggle in Trinidad which had erupted in strikes and violence. Garvey backed the Colonial Office and in so doing had angered Padmore. The final irony is that, when Garvey did die, on June 10th, there was no mention in the *Gleaner* at all.

Next to the proclamation that Garvey was dead, in the May 18th edition of the *Gleaner*, was another story about the Germans invading France and the devastation to life and property being brought about by the Second World War. This was a European war and really exposed any pretence that Europe was the last bastion of sanity and civilisation. In a speech in 1921 called 'White Man Has Spoiled Civilization', Garvey explains his fears: "The white man, who has been the custodian of civilization for the last few hundred years, has spoiled it. You know there are times when you give a contractor a plan after the work has been drawn out splendidly by the architect, and he spoils the job. Haven't you seen that happen?" He goes on: "Therefore, we say what is needed now is a conference of humanity — all humanity — white, black, brown, yellow, red or of whatsoever other color may be found (laughter); a conference of all, and it is for the white man to admit that he has spoiled the plan. Let us help him to execute it well. If he refuses to admit that he has spoiled the plan we cannot afford to allow him to continue spoiling the plan to our disadvantage. (cries of no)."

One of the ironic moments that Amy Ashwood experienced in London, was a final chance meeting with Garvey in Hyde Park. Ashwood, having found her way to Britain, had opened a restaurant on New Oxford Street, near to the British Museum. It operated as a place where black people in London gathered together. Ashwood's meeting with Garvey was set against the background of years of intense bitterness which divided them from the time of their separation in 1920 in America.

She says of her final meeting with Garvey. "I can vividly recall the last occasion when I saw Marcus Garvey. It was shortly before the outbreak of World War II. I watched him walking along Hyde Park, London. He was leaning heavily on his stick, making his way to his special 'soap box' to arouse a curious crowd with the power of his oratory – an art in which he was a maestro. When he caught sight of me he made a magnificent effort to recapture the dynamic gait of earlier years. Drooping shoulders were straightened and he mounted the platform in the manner of the old Liberty Hall days. He tried hard to recapture the power of those days, but, alas, it was too late. The old fire has gone."

We are left with the pitiful picture of a sad, isolated and broken man.

Opposite page:
The 'Daily Gleaner' announcing Garvey's death when the man was still alive. The report was sent from New York and his death was just reported in the 'Chicago Defender'.

Washing up in the country. The laundry is spread out on the grass to dry. Garvey grew up in the hard realities of the Jamaican countryside but it did instill a spirit of independence that would be invaluable for his later work.

Early Days

Garvey was born in the Parish of St Ann, Jamaica, the same parish that would later give the world a more lyrical hero in the person of Bob Marley and was reported to be the first place where Columbus landed in 1494.

Garvey describes his town, St Ann's Bay, as being one of the most beautiful areas on earth, nestled on Jamaica's North Coast. Garvey was born on August 17th, 1887; he was the last of 11 children, all of whom died in childhood with the exception of his sister, Indiana. Jamaica had celebrated emancipation in 1838 after years of slavery, where the majority black population had been forcefully taken from West Africa to be the property of white landowners, who then ran Jamaica like a sugar factory. Garvey's parents, Marcus and Sarah, were better off than the average family. His father was a stonemason and strongly independent. Marcus loved St Ann's Bay. Years later he would write ''I was born in the beautiful Parish of St Ann, near the falls of the Roaring River. I grew with nature and drank much of her inspiration.''

Garvey's parents, although peasants, owned land and property and Garvey developed an independent spirit, quickly getting a job in the local printery. He describes this important experience in an autobiographical essay: ''I became a printer's apprentice at an early age, while still attending school. My apprentice master was a highly educated and alert man. In the affairs of business and the world he had no peer. He taught me many things before I reached twelve, and at fourteen I had enough intelligence and experience to manage men. I was strong and manly, and I made them respect me. I developed a strong and forceful character, and have maintained it still.'' At 14 (at the turn of the century) Garvey had an experience that changed his life and took him into the twentieth century a radically enlightened young man. He recalls: ''To me, at home in my early days, there was no difference between white and black. One of my father's properties, the place where I lived most of the time, was adjoining that of a white man. He had three girls and one boy. All of us were playmates. We romped and were happy children playmates together. The little white girl whom I liked most knew no better than I did myself. We were two innocent fools who never dreamed of a race feeling and problem.'' He goes on: ''As a child, I went to school with white boys and girls, like all other Negroes. We were not called Negroes then. I never heard the term Negro used until I was fourteen. At fourteen my little white playmate and I parted. Her parents thought the time had come to separate us and draw the color line. They sent her and another sister to Edinburgh, Scotland, and told her that she was never to write or try to get in touch with me, for I was a 'nigger'. It was then that I found for the first time that there was some difference in humanity, and that there were different races, each having its own separate and distinct social life.''

Garvey's proud peasant independence along with his new found race awareness was to prove critical in his development. At 18, Garvey had an excellent position as manager of a large printing establishment but he had other matters on his mind. ''I started'' he says, ''to take an interest in the politics of my country, and then I saw the injustice done to my race because it was black, and I became dissatisfied on that account. I went travelling to South and Central America and parts of the West Indies to find out if it was different there, and again I found the same situation. I set

The Garvey house on Market Street. Here Garvey lived with his family before moving to Kingston.

sail for Europe and although different it was the same stumbling block — 'You are black.' I asked, 'Where is the black man's government?' 'Where is his King and his kingdom?' 'Where is his President, his country, and his ambassador, his army, his navy, his men of big affairs?' I could not find them, and then I declared: 'I will help to make them'."

On his return, he established himself in Kingston, Jamaica's capital. Although black people outnumbered whites 20 to 1 in the city, they were still full of self-hatred. There is a saying which still holds currency in today's Jamaica which goes: 'Nayga can't bear to see Nayga prosper." The centre of Jamaican life was at King's House, residence of the colonial governor. After the 1865 Morant Bay rebellion, the old representative system, which had at least restrained the governor, was abolished mainly because the local whites feared a black revolution. Britain reluctantly took back the reins of power and ruled the colony directly until the turn of the century.

Despite this, Garvey enjoyed Kingston. People there were politically aware and he frequently joined groups of friends for discussions on local and world affairs by the seaside at Victoria Pier on Saturday nights. He involved himself in social and community work and joined the Printers Union (one of the earliest trade unions in the British West Indies). When the Union went on strike, the bosses offered Garvey favourable treatment not to participate — he sided with the workers and was elected strike leader. Eventually he lost his job but got another in the Government printery.

It was not long before Garvey became a well known figure around Kingston. In addition to his involvement in workers' struggles and social work, he also began to participate in public speaking. He took elocution lessons and visited churches to study the speaking styles of ministers. In later years Garvey would be widely acclaimed as one of the world's greatest orators.

A maths class outside, for some of the children of St Ann's Bay Primary School. Resources are limited in these schools and not much has changed since Garvey's day. Some pupils do remarkably well given the scarce learning resources available to them.

St Ann's Bay Primary School near the site of Garvey's old school, the Principal still has records of Garvey's registration and progress.

A school register, which shows his first day at this school, at the age of ten. A slight oversight, by his teacher gives his birth to be on August 7.

Another lifelong activity that Garvey began in Kingston was journalism. He worked on two newspapers and in around 1910, published a third which was called *Watchman*.

He also became assistant secretary of a pioneer Jamaican political organisation, the National Club. His involvement here can be described as his first practical introduction to anti-colonial politics. The National Club, discontent with the way that British colonialism restricted opportunities for most Jamaicans — politically, educationally and economically — campaigned for more self-government for Jamaicans.

By 1910 it was apparent that Marcus Garvey was going places. Still only 23 years old, he had already made a name for himself as a printer, journalist, orator, social worker, and political activist.

At 23, and off on his explorations, Garvey made Costa Rica his first stop. His uncle got him a job as a time-keeper on a banana plantation. The conditions he found the migrant workers labouring under outraged him and he vainly protested to the British Consulate to be told that they could do nothing about the situation. It seemed that there was no-one to protect the workers' interests. Together with Simon Aguileria, a fellow activist, Garvey started a newspaper, called *La Nacion*, as a means of reaching the immigrants and getting them organised. This was an effective move and soon the Costa Rican and British authorities grew suspicious of him, viewing him as a troublemaker.

From Costa Rica he systematically travelled through West Indian immigrant communities in South America. He visited Guatemala, Nicaragua, Ecuador, Chile, Peru and in Panama he went to the provinces of Bocas del Toro and Colon. The racist treatment and savage exploitation meted out to his people spurred him on to further political and journalistic activity.

Indiana Garvey (Garvey's sister) and her daughter Ruth, whom Garvey adored.

In Panama, he published another newspaper, called *La Prensa*. Garvey returned to Jamaica, in the words of Amy Jacques, "sickened with fever, and sick at the heart over appeals from his people for help on their behalf," — but he did not linger long.

Garvey's sister, Indiana, had gone off to England as a governess to the children of a wealthy Jamaican family and, with her help in 1912, Garvey made England his next stop. The following two years added further to his personal and political development. He found employment on the docks at London, Liverpool and Cardiff, and attended lectures in Law at Birkbeck College in London. He also visited Speakers Corner at Hyde Park, which fascinated him and it was not long before he himself became a soapbox orator. He continued his journalistic activity in England, writing articles which appeared in various publications. He also frequently visited the public galleries at the House of Commons to observe the debates in the parliament which controlled the destiny of the British West Indies and the rest of the Empire.

While in England, Garvey took the opportunity to travel around the British Isles and to Europe. By July 1913, however, his financial resources began to run dry, but he was saved from destitution by a job that he was offered at the *Africa Times and Orient Review*. The magazine was both Pan-African and Pan-Oriental. Its scope included most of what is now referred to as the Third World. An article written by Garvey appeared in the October 1913 issue. It was entitled 'The British West Indies in the Mirror of Civilization' and is the earliest of his published articles available to historians at the present time. It began: "In these days . . . . . when democracy is spreading itself over the British Empire, and the peoples under the rule of the Union Jack are freeing themselves from hereditary lordship, and an

At the age of 14 Garvey was sent as an apprentice to his godfather Alfred Burrows who was a printer in St Ann's Bay. Garvey learnt quickly and soon became an expert printer. The family business continues – this is the grandson of Alfred Burrows. The press that he is operating is the same one that Garvey used during his apprenticeship.

Booker T. Washington: Garvey shared with Washington a deep commitment to the goal of racial improvement. Garvey read Booker T. Washington's autobiography, 'Up From Slavery' which was a major influence on his development. Washington had worked his way to become founder of Tuskegee Institute in Alabama, the most famous black-controlled educational establishment in the world.

unjust bureaucracy, it should not be amiss to recount the condition of affairs in the British West Indies, and particularly, in the historic island of Jamaica, one of the oldest colonial possessions of the Crown.''

Garvey concluded his article with two prophesies: the first, regarding West Indian federation, stated that ''There have been. . . . several movements to federate the British West Indian Islands, but owing to parochial feelings nothing definite has been achieved. Ere long this change is sure to come about because the people of these islands are all one. They live under the same conditions, are of the same race and mind, and have the same feelings and sentiments regarding the things of the world.''

On the second, in relation to the future of the African race, and the role which West Indians play within it, Garvey says: "As one who. . . . knows the people well, I make no apology for prophesying that there will soon be a turning point in the history of the West Indies; and that the people who inhabit that portion of the Western Hemisphere will be the instruments of uniting a scattered race who, before the close of many centuries, will found an Empire on which the sun shall shine as ceaselessly as it shines on the Empire of the North today."

Garvey had run into financial problems again by May 1914 but within a month had saved sufficient money to leave England. He left the port of Southampton on June 8th 1914 arriving in Jamaica on July 18th. Since he had last set foot in Jamaica, he had travelled through Central and South America, Britain and Europe. He had lived in black communities, worked among the people and shared their joys and sorrows. He had agitated on their behalf and noted their weaknesses.

Garvey, while still in London, had read Booker T. Washington's autobiography, 'Up From Slavery'. Born a slave in the US, Washington had worked his way to become founder of Tuskegee Institute in Alabama, the most famous black controlled educational establishment in the world. In the field of politics, he had become the most powerful black man in America. In ways big and small, he had been able to help large numbers of his people.

'Up From Slavery' had a tremendous impact on Garvey. He then and there realised his calling: ''Becoming naturally. . . restless for the opportunity of doing something for the advancement of my race, I was determined that the black man would not continue to be kicked about by all the other races and nations of the world, as I saw in the West Indies, South and Central America, and Europe, and as I read of it in America.''

Perhaps Garvey's greatest influence during this period was Dr Robert Love, who gave Garvey his elocution lessons. Dr Love was Jamaica's leading black politician at the turn of the century. He was born in the Bahamas and worked in the United States for many years. He had also served as a clergyman in Haiti.

He is best remembered for his militant journalism in the *Jamaican Advocate* (1894–1905) but he had also been the main organiser of black representation in the colonial legislature, which was dominated by white planters, merchants, and colonial officials. Love's electoral struggles were bitterly opposed by whites and mulattoes. Most of the black population was disenfranchised. But Love firmly intended to make use of certain limited reforms that had been introduced in 1895. He was elected to the Kingston City Council in 1898 and to the Legislative Council in 1906.

The carve up of Africa had ended in the 1880s with the major European powers each having their slice. It was Love's reaction to what had happened in Africa which led to his being seen as an anti-colonial fighter. He observed. "Africa. . . has been the carcass upon which the vultures of Europe have descended and which

Dr Robert Love who was a major influence on Garvey, believed that mass support could be created by publishing newspapers. Love himself had been a main organiser, at the turn of the century, for black representation in the colonial legislature, which was dominated by white planters, merchants, and colonial officials.

they have sought to partition among themselves, without any regard whatever for the rights of the Africans.''

Garvey was later to say that ''much of my early education in race consciousness is from Dr Love. One cannot read his *Jamaica Advocate* without getting race consciousness. . .if Dr Love was alive and in robust health, you would not be attacking me, you would be attacking him. . .''

If Dr Robert Love represented the secular form of anti-colonialism, then Alexander Bedward (1859–1930) led the clergy's attack. He was a Baptist preacher, who had his church on the banks of the August Town river from where he preached against British colonialism. He said: ''There is a white wall and a black wall, and the white wall has been closing around the black wall; but now the black wall has become bigger than the white wall. Let them remember the Morant War.''

Although Love and Bedward are rooted in the same belief of anti-colonialism their branches of influence are different. Bedwardism attracted the poorest section of the Jamaican peasantry from which the Rastafarians were later to come. Love tended to attract the better off blacks whose advancement was halted by the wall of racism and colonialism.

Alexander Bedward under armed guard. Characteristically speaking in parables as so many Jamaican working people do, Bedward was challenging the colonial state. He modelled his rebellion on the last great Jamaican revolt in 1865 made by Paul Bogle, known as the Morant Bay rebellion. Bogle had ordered the black constables sent out to arrest him, to join their own colour and 'cleave to the black'.

Edward Wilmot Blyden, who was without doubt the finest black intellectual during the nineteenth century. What is sad is the fact that so few people know about him or can get hold of his writings. There is a definite need for his writings to be republished and made available to everyone.

A third crucial influence on Garvey was Edward Wilmot Blyden. I was introduced to his works by Dr Rupert Lewis at the University of the West Indies. Reading two of Blyden's essays gave more than a clue as to why Garvey was to see him as one of the most significant influences of the twentieth century. Blyden has been described as the greatest black intellectual of the nineteenth century. He was born in St Thomas, Virgin Islands and emigrated to Liberia in 1851, where he was appointed Professor of Classics at Liberia College. Blyden concentrated his mind and writings on demonstrating that Africa had once been the artistic, scientific and intellectual leader of the world. He saw the danger posed by the European powers, waiting to take a slice of Africa; he argued for African unity based on what he called the 'African Personality' which links all Africans at home and abroad and can override tribal and religious difference. Clearly these ideas were a major influence on the young Garvey who was an avid reader of the works of Blyden.

Garvey says in a pamphlet written in 1919 called 'The Negro Race — Its Problems?', "You who do not know anything of your ancestry will do well to read the works of Blyden, one of our historians and chroniclers, who has done so much to retrieve the lost prestige of the race, and to undo the selfishness of alien historians and their history which has said so little and painted us so unfairly. Dr Blyden is such an interesting character to study that I take pleasure in reproducing the following passages from his 'Christianity, Islam and the Negro Race.': 'There was, for a long time, in the Christian world considerable difference of opinion as to the portion of the earth and the precise region to which the term Ethiopia must be understood as applying. It is pretty well established now, however, that by Ethiopia is meant the continent of Africa, and by Ethiopians, the great race who inhabit that continent. The etymology of the word points to the most prominent physical characteristics of this people.

"'To anyone who has travelled in Africa, especially in the portion north of the equator extending from the West Coast to Abyssinia, Nubia and Egypt, and embracing what is known as the Nigritian and Soudanic countries, there cannot be the slightest doubt as to the country and people to whom the terms Ethiopia and Ethiopian, as used in the Bible and by the classical writers, were applied.'

"Blyden went on to say the greatest 'religious reforms the world has ever seen. Jewish, Christian, Mohammedan — originating in Asia have obtained consolidation in Africa. And as in the days of Abraham and Moses, of Herodotus and Homer, so today, there is a constantly accessible highway from Asia to the heart of Soudan. Africans are continually going to and fro between the Atlantic Ocean and the Red Sea.' He goes on: 'Science, in its latest wonders has nothing to show equal to the sum of the wonderful things even now seen in Africa. In Africa stands that marvellous architectural pile the great Pyramid which has been the admiration and despair of the world for a hundred generations. Scientific men of the present day, mathematicians, astronomers and divines, regard it as a sort of key to the universe — a symbol of the profoundest truths of science, of religion, and of all the past and future history of man.'"

Under the influences of Washington, Love, Bedward and Blyden, Garvey began to envisage a great movement – a movement to begin to make concrete his developing ideas.

Amy Ashwood remembered how Garvey's Universal Negro Improvement Association began. She had decided to rent a house at 36 Charles Street, Kingston and half of it was put at the disposal of the UNIA for use as a meeting place. It was here that she, Garvey and a few enthusiasts began to elaborate the aims and principles of their association. She said: "We were laying the first foundations of what was to grow into a world-wide mass Negro movement."

Ashwood was to leave Jamaica in 1916 for Panama, to further the work of the spreading of the movement, but she continued to correspond with Garvey throughout the time they were apart. "Dearest Marcus" she wrote "yours safely...to hand and contents carefully noted. I was much surprised at your long silence. Why it is that you keep my letters so long to answer? I know there is a direct boat every week from New York......

"I don't think it's dear for my mouth, you see Marcus, I have extracted 15 teeth and I lost five previous to that and it's 20 teeth in all. It really isn't dear. It will be done just as good as over there. This is an American and English graduate. I could never pass through Jamaica like this. In fact, I can scarcely talk now without them. And you must write a nice letter as we are related to the effect that you will meet us in New York, or that you will send your wife to meet us. That letter must be showed up at the ticket office before we can get passage. I want you to send next month a pair of high top bronze boots for me and my travelling dress. I want a coat-suit-black silk and a hat to match, but the hat must be toque. Ask for toque, a small hat but my head is very large. I won't worry you for anything after that. My measurement is: Bust-36, Hips-42, Waist-26, Length of skirt-33."

The beautiful Amy Ashwood There was much pomp and ceremony at her marriage to Garvey – she claims that the divorce was never legal.

In the spring of 1918, Ashwood became reunited with Garvey in New York and they were married in 1919. Ashwood had been originally introduced to Garvey by another Amy (Amy Jacques), who was later to become his second wife. As a young man, Garvey had first known Amy Jacques; she was a brown middle-class girl studying to be a legal secretary. The marriage between Ashwood and Garvey ended, after only one year, in 1920, amid a sour conflict concerning unfaithfulness — Ashwood, to her death, felt that she was the woman spurned and accused Jacques of orchestrating the break-up of the marriage. According to Ashwood, when she and Garvey left for America, Jacques wrote to her asking if she could come to America also to help with the secretarial work of the organisation. Amy Ashwood was not keen on book-keeping — her strength was in being out there and talking. She was in fact a great orator and had beaten Garvey at speech contests in Jamaica. The chance to relinquish some of the administrative duties was attractive to Ashwood and she was glad also to have her friend come over — after all, they were both Jamaicans. When Amy Jacques arrived, she pulled everything together in the office and set up more efficient systems. It was then that (according to Ashwood) Jacques decided that Garvey had been her man from the first. Ashwood claims that her hospitality and friendliness towards men was engineered by others into her downfall. Jacques apparently told Garvey that his wife was a 'mule' — a Jamaican expression for a woman who is unable to bear children — and that she was having a liaison with someone else. To prove her case, Jacques arranged for Garvey to burst in on Ashwood one evening, to find her sitting on a couch with a gentleman, both eating sandwiches. Garvey subsequently sued for divorce, but Ashwood claimed that the divorce was illegal as she was out of the country and did not ever sign any divorce papers. Ashwood was left feeling that she had been betrayed both by Garvey and her erstwhile friend, Amy Jacques.

Amy Jacques Garvey: She married Marcus Garvey in 1922, after being his private secretary.

AMERICAN DREAM

Garvey returned to Jamaica after his travels and in 1914 he founded the Universal Negro Improvement Association, or UNIA. The organisation was set up to improve the conditions of black people all over the world, be they in America, the West Indies or Africa. Sadly Garvey found it extremely difficult to make headway with the UNIA in Jamaica, where he felt there was no clear race consciousness. He says: "Men and women as black as I, and even more so, had believed themselves white under the West Indian order of society." By 1916, however, he felt that the black American would respond to his call for racial action. He had heard how they as a people had been totally devastated by the slave experience. The difference between the Jamaican slave experience and the American, is described by Amy Bailey, who was an active member of Garvey's movement and still maintains today that it was this difference that made Garvey leave Jamaica. She says: "Marcus use to say to me that in Jamaica, we thought we had suffered. But it was not a total suffering, our souls had not gone through the mill. For blacks in America the iron went into their souls through their slavery, but in Jamaica it did not go so far. The American Negro would therefore cry out in his spirituals to be able to walk around God's heaven. In Jamaica we have no spirituals, we have folk-songs where we laugh at each other." She continues: "The white man stripped the blackman in America of his inner dignity. The English were born colonisers, they knew it was a mistake to strip the person of the 'I am' within you. He wouldn't say to you, you can't have this job because you are a nigger. He would say I'm sorry but the vacancy is filled. That bitterness never entered the soul of Jamaican slaves."

The American Negro spiritual 'Go Down, Death' tells the story of the suffering black man, whose only release seems to be in the freedom of God's heaven.

Go Down, Death

Oh, de sperrit say: I want you for to
Go down death, easy.
I want you go down death, easy,
I want you go down death, easy,
An bring my servant home.
Go down, death, go down
Preach my glory and mighty name
I want you go down, I want you go down
An bring my servant home.
Oh, de sperrit say: I want you for to
Step to de graveyard easy,
I want you step to de graveyard easy,
I want you step to de graveyard easy,
An bring my servant home.
Oh, de sperrit say: I want you for to
Pass over hell-flames easy,
I want you pass over hell-flames easy
I want you pass over hell-flames easy
An bring my servant home.
Oh, de sperrit say: I want you for to
March up in de Kingdom easy,
I want you march up in de Kingdom easy,
I want you march up in de Kingdom easy,
An bring my servant home.

Previous page:
Garvey at the high point of his mission. He is given Presidential status as he is driven through New York — bodyguards at hand.

By contrast, in Jamaica there were many folk–songs which had a different tone to the spirituals and were used as songs for ring-games.

Dis Long Time Gal

Dis Long time gal a nevva see you
come mek me hol' yu han'
Dis long time gal a nevva see you
come mek me hol' yu han'.
Chorus:
Peel head John Crow si dung pan tree top
Pick off de blossom
Mek me hol' yu han' gal mek me hol' yu han'.
Coda:
Mek me wheel an' turn till we tumble dung
Mek me hol' yu han gal
Mek we wheel an turn till we tumble dung
Mek me hol' yu han' gal.

Jamaican music, however, does not stop with the ring-games. While black American popular music developed into soul and disco, Jamaican music became serious when it moved into reggae, deriving content and inspiration from the philosophy of Rasta.

The Universal African Legion on parade. The UNIA had several auxiliaries and the UAL was one of them. They wore military outfits on horseback and on foot.

For Garvey, Jamaica could never have been the base from which to lead his international programme. He later said to Amy Bailey: "Jamaica will have to learn the hard way. She can't break her own people and get away from it. It will come back to her, you can't do that type of iniquity and get away from it." He was not pointing the finger of accusation at the mass of black people — but at the brown elite who ruled Jamaica with arrogance and insensitivity.

For Garvey, America seemed the right place; he even contemplated marrying an American (Henrietta Vinton Davis, who became his International Organiser). He later said of America that it was ready for him because: "In America the Negro being a minority, in a majority population, realizes immediately that he is classified as an inferior race, and as such he is ostracized and kept back, and sometimes kicked and killed because of his racial attachment. This action has helped to give the American Negro a consciousness that means much to him as a race, and so if anything worthwhile is to come out of the Negro, such will be traceable to the American Negro; except if the West Indian Negro, by some miracle or otherwise can develop a consciousness in his present environment, which will give him the opportunity to prove of really what mettle he is made of as a Negro."

Garvey's arrival and early stay in America would have also coincided with the return of black soldiers from fighting in the First World War. The war itself meant that approximately 370,000 black soldiers served in the US Armed Forces. These soldiers were fighting for democracy and the American dream. But on their return the dream quickly dissipated and the soldiers faced instead a nightmare with many being lynched and suffering awful discrimination. The cases of Henry Johnson and Needham Roberts showed the pain and 'madness' that black American soldiers had to face on their return. They were soldiers of the 15th National Guard of New York and the 369th Infantry; they fought off a raiding party of 24 Germans without any assistance, despite their serious wounds. Johnson became a hero, resisting his assailants with only a knife. Both men received the French Croix de Guerre medal. Johnson subsequently went on a lecture tour throughout New York and St Louis, during which he strongly criticised white soldiers for their cowardice and racism, singling out the Marines particularly, for their refusal to fight in the same trenches as black soldiers. Johnson soon faced arrest on a federal warrant for a technical charge of wearing his uniform beyond the prescribed date. After this incident, perhaps not strangely, he retracted his earlier statements after the hounding he had received from the authorities. On his return to New York he was unable to find work and ultimately was forced to rely on charity.

Garvey later takes up this issue and chastises the white world for its hypocrisy: "During the world war, nations were vying with each other in proclaiming lofty concepts of humanity. 'Make the world safe for democracy, self-determination for smaller peoples,' reverberated in the capitals of warring nations opposed to Germany. Now that the war is over we find these same nations making every effort by word and deed to convince us that their blatant professions were mere meaningless platitudes never intended to apply to Earth's darker millions."

Garvey took full advantage of the new situation and the anger it engendered — black people were not adopting passive positions but were, instead, fighting back. In the years 1917–1919 there were several serious riots against racism.

Thirty-nine blacks and nine whites were killed in the East St Louis riot which erupted on July 2nd, 1917. The black population in the town had increased from around 6,000 in 1910 to almost 13,000 in 1917. The local Democratic Party had

Henrietta Vinton Davis, international organiser of the UNIA.

been able to successfully use the race issue in the 1915 election to discredit the Republicans, whom they accused of importing blacks to increase their electoral power and to use as strike breakers. The local press also encouraged anti-black sentiment in the winter of 1916–17. Violence first occurred on May 28th, 1917 following rumours that a group of blacks killed a white man. Several blacks were injured in the ensuing attacks but there were no deaths. Neither the mayor nor the law enforcement authorities, however, took precautions against further confrontations and in the following weeks both blacks and whites armed themselves for conflict. The culmination of these events came on July 2nd when the streets exploded in violence. The subsequent coroner's inquest on the riot laid the blame for the deaths on the corrupt administration of Mayor Hollman and on the inaction of the police department and the Illinois National Guard.

Garvey took up the issue in a speech the next week entitled: 'The Conspiracy of the East St Louis Riots'. He says: ''The East St Louis Riot, or rather massacre, of Monday will go down as one of the bloodiest outrages against mankind for which any class of people could be held guilty . . . Millions of our people in the early days of slavery gave their lives that America might live. From the labours of these people the country grew in power, until her wealth today is computed above that of any two nations. With all the services that the Negro gave he is still a despised creature in the eye of the white people, for if he were not to them despised, the 90,000,000 of whites of this country would never allow such outrages as the East St Louis massacre to perpetuate . . . Mayor Hollman of East St Louis is a man to be blamed for the recent riots in East St Louis. I say so because I am convinced that he fostered as well as arranged a conspiracy to prevent blackmen migrating from the South, much to the loss of Southern farmers who for months have been moving heaven itself to prevent the exodus of the labour serfs of the South in the North.''

An editorial from the *New York Sun*, 'A lesson from East St Louis' bemoans weak policing. ''When the inevitable eruption of disorder occurred, the police, enervated by a long course of lax discipline and weakened by the system under which they were trained, were unfit to handle it. The county government apparently collapsed utterly. And when the State was compelled to intervene, it sent only 100 troops, and these it dispatched without ammunition for their rifles!''

On the same day as the St Louis riot, Garvey, in a meeting, made reference to the second half of the editorial which read: ''They are doing it in England too. 'Race Rioting in London; Negroes' Homes Mobbed. Caused By White Girls' Infatuation For Black Men, Officer Testifies.' London, July 2nd, 1917 — In consequence of the infatuation of white girls for black men in this district some of the inhabitants are greatly incensed against colored men, said a police officer testifying today in West Ham Police Court adding: 'On Saturday night a gang of youths attacked a number of houses on the Victoria Dock Road where black men lived. Windows were broken and the colored people came into the streets with knives and forks, and one had a revolver. Missiles were thrown by the English lads, and great damage was done.'

''Disturbances lasted until Sunday evening, when a large force of police were drafted into the neighbourhood. A crowd of about 1,000 people had then assembled and stones, sticks, bottles, pokers and tongs were used on both sides. A number of arrests were made.

''A colored man who appeared with his head in bandages was remanded, and several other men, some in bandages, were fined or discharged.''

Garvey referred to this incident as an example of the increasing need for the black man to have a place of refuge — Africa — as white people will always take advantage of a disunited black race.

Garvey was thus forced to change his concept of the UNIA, from an organisation that concerned itself with self-improvement and black excellence, to one with a more radical approach, necessary to deal with the realities of lynching, Jim Crowism and disenfranchisement. Garvey managed to appeal to the large cross-section of black America from peasants to small businessmen. Unlike the situation in Jamaica where shade gradations dominated colour consciousness, in the US a drop of African blood made you a 'Negro'; the UNIA therefore, had mixed-race and near whites within the movement — something that would be unheard of in Jamaica. Thus, Garvey arrived on to an American scene which was more than ready for him. He brought with him the drive for self-governance of the Caribbean peasantry and merged it with the racial consciousness and search for justice of the black American people. It is this that became the essence of what we know as Garveyism; his individual qualities of leadership, derived from his background, were also an important factor.

Claude McKay: Jamaican writer who lived in America. He was moved to write war poems after the First World War as black soldiers faced racism and lynching.

The post-war bitterness struck deep and so created the conditions for Garvey's rise. Those affected by this bitterness included political activists and also many Harlem artists. Some of them became drawn to Garvey, like the Jamaican poet and novelist Claude McKay. McKay was an outstanding cultural figure and a leader among those responsible for that outpouring of writing by blacks in the United States in the 1920s, known as the Harlem Renaissance. His autobiographical writings give a vivid first hand account of the conditions which led many to convert to Garveyism. As a young man in Jamaica, McKay worshipped the British Empire and, coming from a well-off background, the bright McKay was influenced by the quaint paternalism of the English aristocrat Walter Jeckyll and the Fabian socialism of the Governor, later known as Lord Sydney Olivier. (Incidentally, Sydney Olivier was the uncle of Laurence Olivier of acting fame.) In Lord Sydney's capacity as governor of Jamaica, it was reported that he faced a riot in Kingston and was saved only by the intervention of Marcus Garvey. Wayne Cooper sums up the colonial McKay very well when he writes: "As an educated youth of black peasant origins, McKay thus displayed to a painful degree the psychological ambivalence inculcated among West Indians under British colonialism. Both the strength and weakness of his dialect poetry flowed from his attempt to embrace his black Jamaican origins, while simultaneously clinging to Britain as a spiritual homeland. He was not an Englishman and could not become one; yet custom and education mandated his adherence to British imperialistic values and traditions."

McKay's journey to the United States was to change all this. His imperialistic illusions were to be shattered. This was almost identical to Garvey's experience of 1916 when he made the same journey. Experience of racial discrimination in the US was the single most important factor in McKay's shift to radicalism. The other decisive factor in his development was the turbulence of the post First World War period coupled with the fate of many black soldiers, who were harassed and some lynched on their return to American soil. In 1919, 76 blacks were lynched in the US. In his autobiography, McKay writes: "The World War ended. But its end was a signal for the outbreak of little wars between labour and capital and like a plague breaking out in sore places, between colored and white, murderous shootings and hangings. Travelling from city to city and unable to gauge the attitude and temper of each one, we Negro railroad men were nervous. We were less light-hearted. We did not separate from one another gaily to spend ourselves in speakeasies and gambling joints. We stuck together, some of us armed, going from the railroad to our quarters all through the dreary ominous nights, for we never knew what was going to happen.

"It was during those days that the sonnet, 'If We Must Die', exploded out of me. And for it the Negro people unanimously hailed me as a poet.''

He goes on to say that it was this experience that drew him to the Garvey movement.

The poem 'If We Must Die', alerts us to the fact that there is another battle for the black soldier to fight when he gets home. Rifles were not even cool, when on arrival home they had to face the enemy of the lynch mob. The poem is a rallying call, not for bravery against Germans but for black soldiers to prepare to fight the battle at home. If you must die at least die fighting the real enemy.

If we must die

If we must die, let it not be like hogs
Hunted and penned in an inglorious spot,
While round us bark the mad and hungry dogs,
Making their mock at our accursed lot.
If we must die, O let us nobly die
So that our precious blood may not be shed
In vain, then even the monsters we defy
Shall be constrained to honour us though dead
O Kinsmen! we must meet the common foe!
Though far outnumbered let us show us brave,
And for their thousand blows deal one death blow!
What though before us lies the open grave?
Like men we'll face the murderous cowardly pack,
Pressed to the wall, dying but fighting back!

Black Muslim activist Malcolm X was another person whose early life was connected with the rise of Garveyism in America. He explained in his autobiography how as a child his father was in perpetual fear for his family because he was a member of Garvey's movement. He recalls a particular incident: "When my mother was pregnant with me, she told me later, a party of hooded Ku Klux Klan riders galloped up to our home... brandishing their shotguns and rifles they shouted for my father to come out. She went on: 'The Klansmen shouted threats and warnings at her that we had better get out of town because 'the good Christian white people' were not going to stand for my father's spreading trouble among the 'good' Negroes of Omaha with the 'back to Africa' preachings of Marcus Garvey.''

Malcolm X describes his father, the Reverend Earl Little, as ''a dedicated organizer for Marcus Garvey's UNIA. With the help of such disciples as my father, Garvey, from his headquarters in New York City's Harlem, was raising the banner of black-race purity and exhorting the Negro masses to return to their ancestral home — a cause which had made Garvey the most controversial black man on earth.''

Most of Malcolm's family had lost their lives through lynchings, including six uncles and, ultimately, his father also. The death of Malcolm's uncles had been the primary impetus to his father being willing to risk his own life to spread the Garvey message. Malcolm describes a typical UNIA meeting to which his father would take him. He says: ''I can remember hearing of 'Adam driven out of the garden into the caves of Europe,' 'Africa for the Africans', 'Ethiopians awake!'. And my father would talk about how it would not be much longer before Africa

Opposite page:
The Cotton Club during the 1920s, the entertainment centre in Harlem, where black musicians, singers and dancers would perform for a white audience.

Hon. Rev. R. H. Tobitt, B.A.,
U.N.I.A High Commissioner

The UNIA members saw themselves as belonging to a government in exile, so they appointed a number of ambassadors. This is Hon Rev Richard Tobitt UNIA High Commissioner for British Guiana.

would be completely run by Negroes, 'by black men' was the phrase he always used. 'No one knows when the hour of Africa's redemption cometh, it will be here." He goes on: "I remember seeing the big shiny photographs of Marcus Garvey that were passed around from hand to hand. My father had a big envelope of them that he always took to those meetings. The pictures showed what seemed to me millions of Negroes thronged in parade behind Garvey riding in a fine car, a big black man dressed in a dazzling uniform with gold braid on it, and he was wearing a thrilling hat with tall plumes. I remember hearing that he had black followers not only in the United States but all around the world, and I remember how the meetings always closed with my father saying several times, and the people chanting after him: 'Up, you mighty race, you can accomplish what you will!'"

Garvey's essential proposition for his black readers and audiences tended to reiterate this latter theme: 'Success' as the basis of equality and recognition. Speaking before a Liberty Hall audience on July 11th, 1920, Garvey looked to his youthful days: "I can recall having read and studied in the same class room with white boys, but up to now none of them has made more of a success in life than I have, on their own initiative. Hence I come to the conclusion that I am as good as any white."

In the same year, America witnessed the First International Convention of the Negro Peoples of the World, organised by Garvey. Held at the famous Madison Square Garden, with delegates from all over the black world, the Declaration of Rights of the Negro Peoples of the World was adopted. It was at this meeting that Garvey was elected President General of the UNIA and the Provisional President of Africa. For Garvey, the major task was to rid Africa of the white colonialist and the UNIA quickly shifted from an organisation for black reform to what Garvey called "a Government in exile."

Garvey ran the UNIA in a disciplined manner, members being given rank in what was a strong hierarchical set up with military connotations. The weekly meetings were packed and were conducted with full pomp and ceremony. It was Garvey's idea that even the poorest should come to the meetings smart, even if it meant putting your pants under your bed, if you could not afford an iron. Poor people were transformed as they put on their smart UNIA uniforms. The following report of a Brooklyn meeting in 1922, which Garvey attended, shows the format of the meetings and the emphasis on formality. It would be on these occasions that Garvey would dispense honours, making people Lords and Ladies. While those in the uniform section would receive equivalent military honours:

Report of Brooklyn UNIA Meeting (Brooklyn 23−24 January 1922)

"What was really a big time for the members of Brooklyn Division of the Universal Negro Improvement Association was the occasion of the visit of His Excellency the Hon Marcus Garvey, Provisional President of Africa, and Lady Henrietta Vinton Davis, International Organizer, on the evening of January 23−24.

"At an early hour on January 23 the building was packed to overflowing by members and friends of this the greatest Negro organization in the world, who were waiting with anxious hearts for the arrival of the distinguished visitors.

"Promptly at 8 o'clock the signal was given that they were near, and the colonel, commanding officer Mr Wilfred F. Brazil, commandeered his uniformed Legions to the entrance, from whence they escorted the dignitaries to our meeting place.

"The hall was fittingly decorated for the occasion with the colours of the Red, Black and Green and the stars and stripes of America.

"It was indeed an impressive militaristic ceremony, when, as they entered the building, the hymn dedicated to His Excellency, entitled 'Hail to the Lord's Anointed' was solemnly played on the piano, while the procession wended its way slowly through the aisle. At the conclusion of this the commanding officer gave his military orders for standing at attention with the military salute, while Mr William R. Miller, executive Secretary of the Brooklyn Division played the Ethiopian National Anthem on the piano. During the playing of this anthem the entire audience stood in silent attention, proving that all minds were engrossed with the thought that Africa shall be free.

"At the end of the anthem the chaplain of the division, the Rev C.Hurley, led the devotional exercises, the people still standing, and at their conclusion the officers and Legions retired while the audience sat. Mr William R.Miller, executive secretary, then introduced the president of the Brooklyn Division and called upon him to read the address of welcome to His Excellency and Lady Henrietta Vinton Davis. This was a well worded address which spoke of the loyalty of the members of the Brooklyn Division to the cause of 'Africa for the Africans' — those at home and those abroad.

"Next followed the musical and literary part of the program, which was as follows:

Recitation, 'Africa Shall Be Free' . . . . .Mr Jerome
Anthem, 'Into Pastures Green' . . . . By the Choir
Piano and violin duet . . . . Mr and Mrs Dowell
Baritone solo 'I Come To Thee' . . . . .Capt Armstrong
Recitation . . . . Master Dowell
Duet, 'Faires' . . . . .Mrs Dowell and Mrs Husbands
Recitation
'Legions of the Hour' . . . . .Corporal Grant
Recitation
'Mother Africa' . . . . .Miss Emma Simmons

"The president then introduced Lady Henrietta Vinton Davis, International Organizer, who said in part — 'Your Excellency, Provisional President of Africa, Lady President of the Brooklyn Division, Legions, Motor Corps and Black Cross Nurses, Officers and members of the UNIA:—

'It is indeed a pleasure for me to be here this evening. As International Organizer

African Legion members on military parade in the streets of New York.

Garvey, the great black General looks on as supporters in New York march past.

I went to California, the beautiful land of sunshine, then to Chicago where I received a royal welcome. I noted that they were progressive there and working in harmony for the redemption of Africa.

'I am here to congratulate the members of Brooklyn division upon their loyalty to this cause, and to our great leader because he is used as an instrument in God's hands, to lead his children to freedom.

'Although we are passing through critical times stand by your colors! Stand by the UNIA! Stand by Marcus Garvey! We know that these are the turbulent and troublesome times, as every Negro knows — not only here in New York, Philadelphia and Baltimore, but wherever Negroes dwell. There is trouble, not brought about by us, but by those conditions of chaos in Europe.

'We have got to show our mettle now, for if we lose this opportunity of showing the world our ability for business it will never come back again.

'Therefore in all our difficulties we should resolve to fight and die for the great principles of this organization.

'As I travel from place to place, from city to city, I find great industrial unrest existing everywhere, and in this unrest I find that Negroes are the first to lose their jobs. This should not be in the spirit of fairness, but it is invariably so. It behoves us therefore to open factories, for the employ of our own people. As long as we depend on the white man for a job, so long will we be his football. The new Negro is tired of that sort of thing, so in the spirit of justice and fair play we must become united for our own welfare. And so our wonderful leader is bringing a plan for Brooklyn Division by which you will be better able to conserve your own money in your own interest.

'Would to God he had been born fifty years ago, because the eyes of the Negro would have been opened long ago. We brought up families and left them to die unprotected, without ever thinking of the future of our children, of our posterity.

Because the white man thinks thus they have a republic. They plan for unborn generations.

'So our leader is spending wakeful nights, planning for the development of his people, of our country, Africa.

'Because we believe that God will provide, we are apt to sit quietly and wait upon God, but we must remember that God helps those who help themselves, and the time is when we must help ourselves here, so that we can better help ourselves when Africa has been redeemed.

'I feel that every Negro should stand firmly and show his stamina now, henceforth and forever. This is the time for true men and women; time to weigh ourselves in the balance.

'These are the times through which we are passing, yet with the characteristic buoyancy of spirit and optimism of the Negro, we shall even go through the valley of the shadow of death, and will fear no evil.'

''The next speaker introduced was His Excellency, the Hon Marcus Garvey, amid tumultous applause, the entire audience standing and the guard of honour with drawn sabres. His Excellency said in part:

'Once more it becomes my pleasure to find myself in your midst. I have come here this evening to speak to you and if possible to inspire you. As members and as friends, and as members of the race, you must have been watching the great work of this organization. The Universal Negro Improvement Association came upon the scene a few years ago with a big program of uniting four hundred millions into one solid body.

'For ages it was said to be impossible; for to unite them men worked, laboured, died without fortunately succeeding.

'But we, in course of time, were able to reach the hearts of millions of our race. And tonight the movement has a following loyal and true; a following loyal and

Liberty Hall, Harlem.

true in the civilized known world. Some of you do not appreciate it, but when I tell you that millions are working for the same cause, not only in New York, but in the 48 States of the Union, every country on this western hemisphere, in Africa, Asia and Europe, then you will realize the great power and worth of the Universal Negro Improvement Association.

'In the space of four years it has made the circuit of the world and planted the Red, the Black and Green wherever Negroes live. Others did not make us; we made ourselves. We are first in the history of the race, with the scope and power to be found in the UNIA.

'You will realize that this movement is being assailed by great forces, but you must also realize that it is only things which are worthwhile that are dreaded by others.

'They desire to suppress this movement because of fear. If the Kaiser and the Central Powers were like Haiti, the powers of the world would not have combined forces to fight them. But because the Germans and Central Powers were so dangerous they brought fear upon the world.

'Let me tell you that the UNIA has the combined forces of the world fighting it, because the program is a free and independent Africa.

'Africa has become the danger sign of the world. All nations are looking to Africa. The bankrupt nations of Europe, unable to rehabilitate themselves through their own countries, are looking to Africa as their hope.

Marcus Garvey and Amy Jacques Garvey

'British East Africa must support Britain, French West Africa must support France with resources to rebuild. Italian Africa must also serve the same purpose.

'Then since this is so every attempt to free Africa must meet with opposition. What organization wants to free Africa?' (Cries of 'The UNIA' from audience.) 'That is why unseen forces of government are fighting us.

'The world took us as a joke when we started. They called us a bunch of illiterate, fanatic Negroes. But as we have stood fast in our principle of 'Africa for the Africans' we have startled the world.

'Tonight as you sit here, so hundreds are sitting in Africa concentrating on the same thought of freeing Africa.

'This evening as I was about to leave the office, a cable came to me from Cape Town, saying 'We are holding the fort — we have stirred Africa.'

'Shall we faint under opposition? And we know how to fight because we fought in France and Flanders, in Egypt and Mesopotamia. Some of us may be faint-hearted, but I say unto you faint-hearted ones, 'You shall die.'

'Brave men shall go and take the colors of the Red, the Black and the Green on the hilltops of Africa.

'We shall not be serfs; we shall be free, we care not what may come! Give me liberty or give me death!

'Some preachers are against us, saying we are too radical. But only radicals will find a place in the sun. The age of turning the right cheek if you are hit on the left is past. This is a Jack Johnson age, when the fittest will survive.

'For over fifty-odd years we had lost hope and heart, because we saw no hope for our ambitions. We saw millions pushing us back. But, thank God Negroes have changed.

'Their ability is being used for the greater glory of Africa. We shall so work that one day we shall be free.

'We shall not be afraid of our own flag in the world. They laugh and say that I am spectacular. Who is more spectacular than the Pope? These are the very people who were laughed at in ages past. The Anglo-Saxons were whipped and serfed

Marcus Garvey was declared Provisional President of Africa.

by Rome. The Britons have risen; so shall the Negro rise to be the proudest nation of the world. We are working for our children.

'You of Brooklyn continue! The fight is long. All true warriors know no fear. Our friends are faint-hearted, but Jesus Christ was the greatest radical the world ever saw. Jesus opposed wrong. His program was to lift up humanity and save mankind.

'We are exhorting our people to rise. And I say uphold your own program. I feel that we are to live out our own program, and march out and do things.

'You must advance our own leadership. We have demonstrated to the world that Negroes are able to carry a program of their own.

'A program of warfare to make us true men indeed.

'Lead out as generals to map out our own course of victory. We are different from others; we have a great program. Why should we allow others the access to all the pleasures of life, and we be as peons, serfs, slaves? Are you not children of the Common Creator? Some don't believe that God made them. Who made you? If God made you and other people, then he made you for an equal purpose — to be lords of creation.

'He could not intend you to worship him in spirit and in truth if you were created to be slaves. God made us his masterpiece — yellow, brown, black, to be equals of all men. If he intended you to have a lower place, he would not have given you the position of being men.

'He would have created you with the lower animals. But 'man' meant equal of all men.

'Then let us make a comparison between white and black men. White men — heads of governments, heads of nations, having towering cities.

'When God created you equal of all he gave you the ability to do things for yourself. That you occupy your present positions is not God's fault but yours. God is vexed with you because you have hidden your talents.

'As other men have built great cities, so will we build them in the great Empire of Africa.

'As other men have the United States of America so shall we build the great United States of Africa. Can it be done?' (Cries of 'yes!') 'Some of you have no hope, no confidence. Willpower is all. Some will to do and some will not to do. Some men will scare death itself to get some desired object. White men willed that the forest shall be cleared for himself and the trees went down. This spot on which this building is erected was a swamp and wilderness hundreds of years ago, today there is a house on it. The Negro must do or die. The man who cannot find his purpose in life ought to die.

'There is a work for each and everyone of us to do in life. You must find it for yourself. Search your consciousness.

'From the time I got sense and was able to read my first duty was to find out what I was best fitted for. And I found out that I am to make trouble in the world' (outbursts of laughter). 'Some of us are fitted to be good musicians, bricklayers, tailors, lawyers. Discover yourself. This is the thought I want to leave with you. Discover yourself. Find it out tonight.

'God never meant you to sweep and carry poles. God made you and was through. It is for you to do the rest. He handed you the world and said: ' You are the Lord of creation. If you want to be drawers of water and hewers of wood, it is your business.' He gave you two hands, two eyes, a head and body, and he was through. If you have no better use for your hands than to be drawers of water and scrub the floors, that is your business. How long will you allow this to be? God never cursed you, you cursed yourself.

'And the UNIA wants to say, No man can make you do what you don't want to do. You do as you like.

'You fought and died for England and France in the name of God and reason, go out and preserve the Republic of Africa for yourselves and for your children. Others have done it you must do it. It must be accomplished.

'The world in which we live is reorganizing. Every race is seeking a place of its own. Japanese are looking for a greater Japan, Indians — a free India, greater India; Egyptian, a free and independent Egypt. The Irish, who had been clamoring for 750 years for a free and independent Ireland, have got an Irish Free State.

'It means that all must realize that we who are unorganized must be and will be the serfs and peons of the stronger of the world.

'While America, England, France are protected throughout the world; so shall we struggle for the protection of our people, wheresoever they may dwell.

'Struggle for a greater Africa, and we accept no compromise. Some preachers and others are too aggressive. How can we sit by? Can we allow it?

'Our fathers suffered because they had no vision. If you have no vision you perish. Our vision must be that of a free and independent African commonwealth, strong enough to protect Negroes everywhere.

'I am going to strive and struggle until Africa is free' (Applause). 'Shall I shut up?' (Cries of 'No'). 'If I should die, and there is any truth about ghosts coming back, I will be one bad ghost until Africa is free.

'Those who are organized to fight us are fighting God because God has said that a princess shall come out of Egypt. And she is now stretching out her hands unto God. No preachers can stand in our way. The UNIA with Jesus as our leader is preparing a program which shall startle the world until we plant the colors of the Red, the Black and the Green upon the battle plains of Africa.'

''The President-General then announced that his subject for Tuesday evening, January 24, will be 'The Call of the Hour' to which all were invited.

''Thus a memorable event in the annals of Brooklyn Division was brought to a close at 11 o'clock p.m.''

But along with the fiery speeches and rapid rise in membership, mistakes were also made by Marcus Garvey. One in particular stands out — his meeting with the Ku Klux Klan. There was also the controversy over the Black Star Line Shipping Corporation which eventually led to his being deported from America.

Garvey has been accused of being a 'racist', others said he was simply naive for having secret meetings in Atlanta with the acting Imperial Wizard of the Ku Klux Klan. In a speech made in New York on July 9th, 1922, Garvey explains why he met with the Klan leader. In his own way Garvey develops an argument for black nationalism in the face of what he sees would otherwise have been an insoluble conflict of interests. Garvey says: "I interviewed the Imperial Wizard of the Ku Klux Klan to find out the Klan's attitude toward the race. You may believe it or not — I made several statements to him, to which he said this: 'That the Klan is not organized for the absolute purpose of interfering with Negroes — for the purpose of suppressing Negroes, but the Klan is organized for the purpose of protecting the interests of the white race in America'."

Garvey goes on to argue that the Klan is a purely racial organisation, which seeks to make America a white man's country while the UNIA wants Africa to be a black man's country. The solution must be, ''That the Negro create a government of his own strong enough on the continent of Africa that can compel the respect of all men in all parts of the world.''

Garvey felt without any doubt that the Klan were more than just a fringe lunatic organisation responsible for lynching black people. He saw them as being the honest or real face of America: ''I prefer and I have a higher regard for the man who intends to take my life who will warn me and say, 'Garvey, I am going to take your life,' so as to give me time to prepare my soul for my God, rather than the man who will pretend to be my friend, and as I turn my back he ushers me into eternity without even giving me a chance to say my Lord's Prayer.'' At another time he says ''Between the Ku Klux Klan and the Moorfield Storey National Association for the Advancement of ''Coloured'' People group, give me the Klan for their honesty of purpose towards the Negro. They are better friends to my race, for telling us what they are and what they mean, thereby giving us a chance to stir ourselves, than all the hypocrites put together with their false gods and religions, notwithstanding. Religions that they preach but will not practise; a God they talk about, whom they abuse every day. Away with the farce, hypocrisy and lie. It smells, it stinks to high heaven.''

A Ku Klux Klan meeting in Alabama. Garvey called the Ku Klux Klan the true face of white America.

He argued that it was pointless attempting to fight the Klan because they not only represent the totality of white America, but the common UNIA desire for the black man to make something of himself, separate from white people.

The Klan leader explained to Garvey: ''We are not organizing to be unfair to the Negro; we want to see the Negro develop as the whiteman has developed. To be fair, I advise every Negro and those who aspire to leadership to form an organisation similar to that of the Ku Klux Klan so that the Negroes may be able to look out for their own interests and not continue to be begging white people to do for them what they ought to do for themselves...''

Although we have the Ku Klux Klan leader sounding like an early version of Louis Farrakhan, Garvey's explanations of his meetings with 'the Imperial Wizard' do not seem convincing. Certainly, on the political level, it was costly; this was shown at the third UNIA convention in 1922 where Garvey repudiated the entire executive council, expressing his anger over plots against him within the UNIA leadership. But although Garvey was able to silence his critics within the UNIA, the price was to be a badly frustrated and demoralised movement. At the same time, his political adversaries outside the UNIA were steadily gaining ground against him.

At the time, Garvey already had a membership world-wide of something approaching 10 million. Through his meetings with the Ku Klux Klan, Garvey did not gain any ground toward his main objective, which was to liberate Africa and gain a Continental base. It seems rather that the exercise resulted in his alienating, and in some cases losing, black support.

But Garvey was living at a time when the black man was meant to feel that he was nothing — he was not only an inferior kind of creature but also a special kind of property. It was, as well, a time when peoples across the world were fighting for identity: the Jews were seeking to establish themselves, likewise the Russians, while the Indians too sought independence; so Garvey considered it necessary for the black man also to find his place in the world. He interpreted the Christian tradition of both Old and New Testament, to accommodate his movement. The primary concern was to put the black man on the map. Linking the Christian tradition with this latter concern, Garvey evinced that the greatest honour for black people to give to God is to see themselves as a masterpiece in the hands of the Lord.

Garvey wanted to show that the "Black man doesn't have to drive cart all him life"; his domain is not confined to the cotton field or the banana plantation but he is capable of running steamships and governing nations.

Garvey conceived his racial mission as the achievement of black success. "Negroes, get busy quickly looking after yourselves and your business." Garvey went on: "And your business is to get as much out of the earth in common with other people as you can." What then is particularly unique about this outlook? Well, Garvey combines this notion of success with the belief in African nationalism. For Garvey, the common denominator for black people is Africa. He points to the historical fact of where the black race truly originates from. He sees slavery as a tragic interruption: "3,000 years ago black men excelled in government and were the founders and teachers of art, science and literature. We can return to it with the rebuilding of Africa. Black men of the highest learning and the highest accomplishments."

Garvey was concerned about the place of black people in the world — that if they did not go forward through their own organisation, their ultimate fate would be extermination. He says: "There is no doubt about it that we are living in the age of world reorganization out of which will come a set program for the organized races of mankind that will admit no sympathy in human affairs."

Garvey argues that: "The new Negro is demanding a place in the affairs of men." He must be able to run his own country and have an empire — a platform. Africa must be free and the blackman ruling. Otherwise would his fate be similar to that of the Red Indian? What had happened to the Red Indian in North America, Garvey saw slowly happening to the black race in Africa. Therefore Africa would be developed by those in the Diaspora returning to Africa and working with the native Africans — to build a strong Africa. This would save the black race from extinction and also avoid what he saw as a war of the races. He says: "There is no other way to avoid the threatening war of the races that is bound to engulf all mankind, which has been prophesied by the world's greatest thinkers; there is no better method than by apportioning every race to its own habitat." He goes

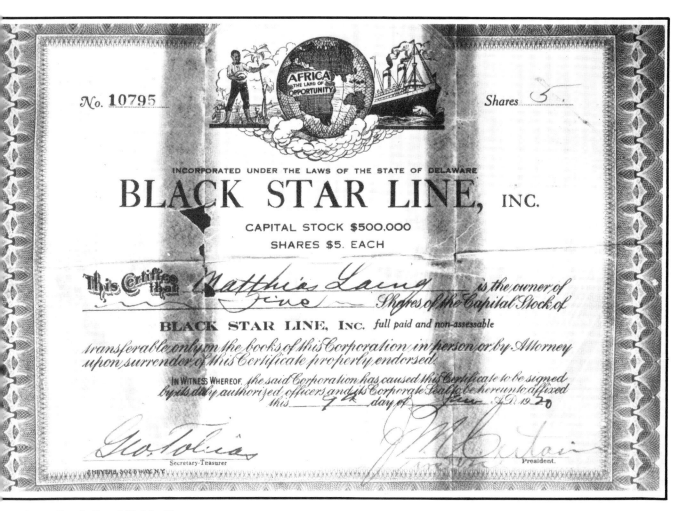

A share certificate for Garvey's Black Star Line Company.

on: "The time has come for the Asiatics to govern themselves in Asia, as the Europeans are in Europe and the Western world, as it is wise for the Africans to govern themselves at home, and thereby bring peace and satisfaction to the entire family." Garvey wanted a black powerbase. It was no coincidence that he would dress as a Field Marshall and have his UNIA members in military garb playing military music. He says: "England, France, Italy, Japan and America attract the attention of the rest of mankind in the quest for Justice, for fair play, when we can produce to the world the 'real stuff', that makes man feel if he doesn't hear."

Garvey's burning desire for success in his mission, culminated in the Black Star Shipping Corporation which was established in October 1919.

For black people to own a modern shipping company at that point in history seemed like an impossible dream to many. Within the first year of its launch more than $600,000 had been raised through stock sales and three ships had been purchased. The Black Star Line was designed to demonstrate what self-reliance could achieve. It was financed by black people who bought shares in the company.

Everywhere the Black Star Line ships docked, they were welcomed in a carnival atmosphere. The ships toured the Caribbean and became for Garvey a symbol of "the possibility of achieving success and glory." Sadly the Black Star Line

The crew of S.S. Yarmouth

proved to be a financial disaster, with the total operations deficit on its three vessels estimated at around $47 million. Garvey was charged with fraud in 1922 when a member continued to advertise shares for sale after the venture had collapsed. Garvey was jailed in 1925 for five years in the Atlanta Federal State Penitentiary, fined $1,000, and ordered to pay the entire cost of the hearing. He argued, in his defence, that companies fail every day and therefore a promise of profit does not necessarily make them fraudulent. However, in a fixed trial, the authorities got Garvey where they wanted him: jailed. One of his failings had been that, as the UNIA had grown, he had neglected to take care with members who had ample opportunity to steal from the company. Sadly, there were many cases of his subordinates deliberately sabotaging ships and stealing money. After a major campaign to bring about Garvey's release, President Calvin Coolidge commuted the sentence and, in November 1927, Garvey was deported back to Jamaica.

While Garvey was imprisoned he had lost his foothold in Liberia. Liberia had held a special attraction for him. The state had been established in 1820 and became the land where American ex-slaves could return if they wanted. It, along with Haiti and Ethiopia, were the only black independent countries. Garvey had hoped to move the UNIA headquarters and several thousand of his followers to Liberia. In 1921 Garvey had managed to sign an agreement which meant that the UNIA could set up a small embassy in Monrovia, the capital, and a group of experts were sent over to begin work on a UNIA settlement. Garvey's fraud case lasted

Captain Joshua Cockburn (seated) E.D. Smith-Green (right) and two Cuban UNIA leaders. Cockburn was ship's captain of The Yarmouth which was launched on October 31st, 1919, she sailed to Cuba with a cargo of cement for Sagua La Grande, Cuba. From Cuba Cockburn informed Garvey that the white engineers had tried to run the ship aground. However, Smith-Green and Cockburn were taking kickbacks which amounted to $8,000.

In February 1925, Garvey was jailed. Garvey is handcuffed to US Marshalls and taken from the Federal Court to the Tombs Prison. A New York attorney remarked that in Garvey's case the defendant was treated with 'manifest unfairness', and with a 'palpable attempt at persecution.'

for three years; while he was fighting it, the American and European colonial powers put pressure on Liberia to break any trading agreement they had made with the UNIA. Meanwhile, the Liberians signed a deal with the Firestone Rubber Company to lease out acres of land for rubber cultivation, thus destroying Garvey's hopes of building an African empire from Liberia.

The shipping line controversy revealed a major weakness in the UNIA, in that it was too dependent on the power and personality of Garvey. Therefore, when Garvey was deported, in 1927, the movement in America was devastated and there was no focus for unity, thus creating a splintering of the organisation and the beginnings of its demise.

However, despite the setback of the KKK meetings and the disaster of the Black Star Line and Garvey's subsequent deportation, the UNIA movement continued in the short term, to grow. At one stage it was estimated that it had a following of 11 million people. There were branches of the UNIA in countries as diverse as Wales, South Africa and Australia.

UNIA Branches in the United States in 1926

State	Number of Branches	State	Number of Branches
Louisiana	74	Alabama	11
Virginia	48	Connecticut	10
North Carolina	47	Maryland	10
Pennsylvania	45	Tennessee	9
West Virginia	44	Texas	9
Mississippi	44	Kentucky	8
Ohio	39	Kansas	7
Arkansas	38	Massachusetts	7
New Jersey	31	Colorado	3
Florida	32	Arizona	4
Oklahoma	28	Delaware	3
Georgia	26	Washington	3
Illinois	23	Iowa	2
South Carolina	24	Columbia	2
Missouri	21	Rhode Island	2
California	16	Nebraska	1
New York	16	Oregon	1
Michigan	14	Utah	1
Indiana	13	Wisconsin	1

Distribution of UNIA branches outside the United States

Country	Number of Branches	Country	Number of Branches
Cuba	52	Canal Zone (Panama)	2
Panama	47	South West Africa	2
Trinidad	30	Wales	2
Costa Rica	23	Antigua	1
Canada	15	Australia	1
Jamaica	11	Bermuda	1
Spanish Honduras	8	Brazil	1
South Africa	8	Dominica	1
British Guiana	7	Dutch Guiana	1
Colombia	6	Equador	1
Dominican Republic	5	Grenada	1
Guatemala	5	Haiti	1
Nicaragua	5	Nevis	1
Barbados	4	Nigeria	1
British Honduras	4	Puerto Rico	1
Mexico	4	St Kitts	1
Sierra Leone	3	St Lucia	1
England	2	St Thomas	1
Gold Coast	2	St Vincent	1
Liberia	2	Venezuela	1
Bahamas	2		

(Figures from Tony Martin's 'Race First').

The figures show Cuba as the biggest supporter of the UNIA outside of the United States. What was unusual was that South Africa was the best organised of all the African countries. It remained a fact that all significant black populations in the world had a UNIA branch. Garvey was a master propagandist — not only did he tour many of these countries, but like all good Presidents he sent ambassadors to encourage the membership. The latter was also achieved through his newspapers, the most important Garvey publication being the 'Negro World', published in Harlem from 1918–1933. Many colonial authorities attempted to ban the newspaper but copies got as far as Australia and South Africa, most often smuggled by black seamen.

The American Legacy

"The need (of blacks) to assert their own definitions, to reclaim their history, their culture; to create their own sense of community and togetherness. There is a growing resentment of the word "Negro", for example, because this term is the invention of our oppressor; it is *his* image of us that he describes. Many blacks are now calling themselves African-Americans, Afro-Americans or black people because that is *our* images, stereotypes — that is, lies — that our oppressor has developed will begin in the white community and end there. The black community will have a positive image of itself that *it* has created. This means we will no longer call ourselves lazy, apathetic, dumb, good-timers, shiftless, etc. Those are words used by white America to define us. If we accept these adjectives, as some of us have in the past, then we see ourselves only in a negative way, precisely the way white America wants us to see ourselves. Our incentive is broken and our will to fight is surrendered. From now on we shall view ourselves as African-Americans and as black people who are in fact energetic, determined, intelligent, beautiful and peace-loving." (Stokely Carmichael and Charles V Hamilton, *Black Power: The Politics of Liberation in America.)*

Marcus Garvey encountered many critics during his American period, but the most bitter rivalry came from one of America's great black intellectuals. W. E. Burghardt DuBois published a book in 1890 called 'The Souls of Black Folk' in which he argued: "One ever feels his two-ness — an American a Negro; two souls, two thoughts, two unreconciled strivings." For DuBois the main problem facing the black man was how to be integrated into American society; he became the most powerful spokesman for the integrationist organisation, the National Association for the Advancement of Coloured People (NAACP). This was formed in 1909 by liberal whites. DuBois in the magazine, *Century*, attacks Garvey and his mentor, Booker T. Washington: "The present generation of negroes," he says "has survived two grave temptations — the greater one, fathered by Booker T. Washington, which said: 'Let politics alone, keep in your place, work hard, and do not complain,' and which meant perpetual color caste for colored folk by their own co-operation and consent, and the consequent inevitable debauchery of the white world; and the lesser, fathered by Marcus Garvey, which said: 'Give up! Surrender! The struggle is useless; back to Africa and fight the white world."

Garvey was motivated by the ideals of service and success coupled with the belief that with sheer guts and determination, the goal of becoming a self-made man was realisable. This was opposed to the aspirations of DuBois, who was no peasant from St Ann's Bay but rather was born into the gentle elegant New England middle class where, being light-skinned, he passed as mulatto. He was a brilliant academic finally going to Harvard. DuBois, however, with his concept of the 'Talented Tenth,' an elite to lead black people into a fully integrated America, had no real appeal to the mass of poor black Americans. Garvey saw himself as the ideal self-made man who had conquered disadvantage and made himself a success through his own heroic struggles. Garvey explains the difference between himself and DuBois thus: "Marcus Garvey was born in 1887; DuBois was born in 1868; that shows that DuBois is old enough to be Marcus Garvey's father. But what has happened? Within the fifty-five years of DuBois' life we find him still

W. E. B. DuBois: At first a bitter rival to Garvey but he eventually takes up a Garveyite perspective.

living on the patronage of good white people, and with the thirty-six years of Marcus Garvey (who was born poor and whose father, according to DuBois, died in a poor house) he is able at least to pass over the charity of white people and develop an independent program originally financed by himself to the extent of thousands of dollars, now taken up by the Negro people themselves. Now which of the two is poorer in character and manhood?''

Garvey later lays down the gauntlet as if they were two prize fighters and says: ''Suppose for the proof of the better education and ability Garvey and DuBois were to dismantle and put aside all they possess and were placed in the same environment to start life over afresh for the test of the better man? What would you say about this, doctor? Marcus Garvey is willing now because he is conceited enough to believe that in the space of two years he would make you look like a tramp in the competitive rivalry for a higher place in the social, economic world.''

Garvey may have appeared rather conceited here but it must be remembered that he was responding to some venomous attacks from DuBois and so, in that sense, he was doing little more than getting even. At one stage DuBois described Garvey as: "A little, fat black man, ugly, but with intelligent eyes and a big head..." More seriously for Garvey, however, DuBois along with the NAACP were part of the 'Marcus Garvey Must Go' campaign, which eventually achieved their aim with his deportation.

DuBois died in Ghana in 1963 at the age of 95. He spent many of his years working out how to overcome racism in America, until ironically he finally arrived at a Garveyite perspective. If I were to write a book on DuBois, I would call it 'W.E.B. DuBois: the reluctant Garveyite'. His eventual conversion would begin in 1930 when Garvey was back in Jamaica, and DuBois moved from integration to separation. Garvey himself was quick to notice the shift — in a headline in his paper, *Negro World*, Garvey declared: "Dr DuBois agrees with UNIA. Leader Takes Program Over Finally — But Does Openly Confess It. Emphasizes Negro Owned Industries, Business."

George Stretor wrote soon after: ''It is significant that the Garvey idea, however much it was ridiculed by Negro intellectuals during the heyday of the movement, has not downed. On the contrary, it reappears in the most unexpected quarter, for example, in the currently expounded DuBois doctrine of a black economy.''

Although DuBois did come round to seeing the world from a Garveyite perspective after becoming completely disillusioned with the integrationist philosophy of the NAACP, it remains one of the tragedies of black history that these two great men did not at any stage work together.

Another person influenced by Garvey was ex-communist George Padmore. He was born in Trinidad (real name Malcolm Nurse). After working for the *Trinidad Guardian*, he became a freelance journalist. An ardent Communist at the time, he was a member of the Communist Party of America and an official of the Communist International. Padmore, as the 'father of African emancipation', clearly became a significant figure. After meeting the young Nkrumah (future President of Ghana) Padmore was to have a great influence on him. Once in power Nkrumah made Padmore head of the Department of African Affairs.

Ghana became the engine room for the struggle for African independence, led and planned under the guiding hand of George Padmore. It was at Padmore's original 1945 Paris International conference, (where anybody and everybody involved in the question of African independence met), that the call came for 'immediate independence'. The British government, now running scared, invited Padmore to a conference in Oxford where matters were to be discussed 'as gentlemen' over sherry. However, the British knew that the sun was setting for colonialism, and Padmore's work helped secure independence for about 40 African states.

Padmore was clearly not, however, always the golden boy of the Garveyite tradition. As a Communist he had bitterly opposed Garvey's anti-communist position. In a message to the *Daily Worker*, Garvey said: "We have sympathy for the Workers Party. But we belong to the Negro party, first, last and all the time. We will support every party that supports us, and we appreciate the attention the Workers Party has given us in sending this friendly communication. But the Communists have a long time ahead of them before they can do anything for themselves in this country. When they get there we will be for them. But meantime we are for ourselves."

Comments like this would infuriate Padmore; in 1931 he attacked Garvey, saying: "The struggle against Garveyism, represents one of the major tasks of the Negro toilers in America and the African and West Indies colonies. Like Zionism and Gandhism, Garveyism is merely out to utilize racial and national consciousness for the purpose of promoting the class interests of the black bourgeoisie and landlords." Reminiscent of the early DuBois, Padmore was to say that Garvey was "the greatest fraud and racketeer who has ever imposed himself upon an oppressed people."

In 1935 everything changed for Padmore when he decided to leave the Communist Party. Trinidadian intellectual C.L.R. James vividly recalls the moment: "I saw him looking somewhat dishevelled and I said, 'George, what up?' He said, 'I have left those people, you know.' It was many months before I got the full significance of that. For him the Communist International was 'those people'. He had been working with them because they wanted someone, and they would spend the money to help the organisation to develop. But he did not believe in them, and he told me why he left them. It is extremely important. They (the Communist leaders) told him, 'Well, George, the situation is changing and we want you now to take it easy with the Democratic Imperialists — Britain, France and the United States — and lead the attack on the Fascist Imperialists Germany, Italy and Japan.'

"Padmore told them, 'But how can I do that? Germany and Japan have no colonies in Africa and the United States is the most race-conscious country in the world? How do you expect me to tell those three in my African propaganda that they are the Democratic Imperialists? So they told him, 'Well, George, you know that is the line.' And in those days when the Communists said that that was the line you followed, or if you got another line, you went out."

During the 1950s Padmore published his major work 'Pan-Africanism or Communism.' In this text he called Garvey "the greatest black prophet and visionary since Negro Emancipation." He admits that it was the Garvey influence that had made him depart from Communism.

Historian C.L.R. James was another critic who changed his mind and admits that he did not fully understand the importance of Garvey until later. He says: "I knew Garvey quite well. He would say, 'Well James, how are you? You and I don't say the same things James, but we are headed in the same direction.' We met, yes, I wouldn't quarrel with Garvey. In my early writings I made some stupid criticisms. Later I realised that Garvey began the movement."

C.L.R. James argues that Garvey brought together the Caribbean, America and Africa and showed that for black people, there is an important historical link. James says: "When Garvey finished, all recognised that black people were a social force. He started us off, for me Garvey was the beginning." He goes on: "Garvey was

Opposite page:
C.L.R. James claims that Garvey changed history.

the first man to make black people aware of themselves as an international force. He said that black history and world history are linked, he basically made blacks part of world history. He told all black people we are one. It was part of the modern conception of world history. History is moving towards 'concentrated' parts — Pan-Arabism, Pan-Europeanism, Pan-Americanism. When Pan-Africa develops — it will turn to Garvey to find its place in the world.''

James shows that prior to Garvey, black people were not part of the world community. His vision had made them part of the progressive world by linking their history with that of the mainstream world. In a similar way, Marx and Engels had changed the way people looked at history, demonstrating that what determined the progress of history was the workers relationship to capital. Lenin and the Russian Revolution had made concrete Marx and Engels' vision. Garvey's ideas had provided a similar catalyst for the struggles of the black man. C.L.R. James explains: "Before Marcus Garvey, there was no black movement. The black movements that we have today all started with him and when you consider what it was, and I know what it was to be a black person in those days — blacks were essentially people who tilled the soil and carried — but for Garvey to come forward and say some of the things he said, that was a tremendous vision. The only person I know who can be compared to what Garvey did is Adolph Hitler. Adolph Hitler came forward and upset the traditions of Western civilisation. They had the growth of democracy, 1789 and everything and Adolph Hitler said 'No! Race and blood matter' and the Germans upset completely the mentality and outlook of Western civilisation."

C.L.R. James qualifies his reference to Hitler: "I am not comparing Garvey to Hitler. I am comparing one historical movement and another historical movement. There were these two men who upset the mental conception of modern history. Marcus Garvey unleashed the revolutionary capacity of blacks and colonial people. When you consider what that did (it was part of the break-up of the 19th century) you realise that Garvey played a tremendous role. Garvey was a great historical figure. The world lived according to certain relations, the world lived up to 1914 in the progressive development of democracy for everybody and the colonial peoples were to develop and in time become democratic. World War 1 finished up with that and Garvey said 'No! All black people and people of colour are going to be free.' Since that time the 20th century is the most disturbed century in the history of mankind and these two were responsible for the break-up."

Speaking before the second UNIA convention, in August 1921, Garvey declared: "All other races are on strike now... Four hundred million Negroes are striking and we are striking now with a vengeance, never to be abused, never to be tossed about, never to be kicked about again, because we have found a way to liberty." In the paper, the *Negro World*, in 1922, UNIA member William Ferris wrote: "The same desire for justice and liberty which De Valera has voiced for Ireland, Mahatma Gandhi for India and Egyptian leaders for Egypt, Marcus Garvey has voiced for Africa."

The bigger black movements in the twentieth century such as Black Power and the Rastafarian movement have strong links with Garveyism in its most productive American phase. However other movements such as liberation theology and the development of workers progressive movements also find inspiration in Garveyism and they, like Malcolm X, Nkrumah, Louis Farrakhan, Patrice Lumumba and Elijah Mohammad, among others, all owe some debt to the thoughts and vision of that small peasant boy from Jamaica.

Malcolm X has for some people been a symbol of race hate and bitterness, but

Opposite page:

Malcolm X. He said: "Every time you see another nation on the African continent become independent you know that Marcus Garvey is alive."

a proper reading of the man shows that he was a leader in the mould of Garvey and he never lost the early Garvey influence to which he had been exposed through his Garveyite father.

The violent death of Malcolm X's father by a lynch mob was for him an abiding memory and motivation to action. "My father's skull on one side" he says, "was crushed in, I was told later. Negroes in Lansing have always whispered that he was attacked, and then laid across some tracks for a streetcar to run over him. His body was cut almost in half. He lived two and a half hours in that condition. Negroes then were stronger than they are now, especially Georgia Negroes. Negroes born in Georgia had to be strong simply to survive."

Like Garvey, Malcolm X had seen the underbelly of 'white America' and like Garvey he felt that so long as one race despised itself and the other thought itself superior, then there would be no peace. He describes the Harlem of the early 1930s, where he worked before his imprisonment, driving upper-class white men to a Harlem brothel where they could fulfil all their fantasies for a fee. He says: "Harlem was their sin den, their fleshpot. They stole off among taboo black people, and took off whatever antiseptic, important, dignified masks they wore in their white world. These men who could afford to spend large amounts of money for two, three, four hours indulging their strange appetites." In Harlem Malcolm X claims that he learnt the soul of the white man and he began to wonder why he had for so long loved white and hated black. He goes on: "Some of them would pay me extra to come and watch them being beaten. That girl greased her big Amazon body all over to look shinier and blacker. She used small, plaited whips, she would draw blood, and she was making herself a small fortune off those old white men."

In 1948 whilst in prison, Malcolm X became a Muslim after hearing about his brother's conversion. He joined the Muslim prophet Elijah Muhammad who claimed to be a hand-picked messenger of Allah. Muhammad was head of the organisation, Nation of Islam, which followed a strict Muslim regime.

The UNIA shared in common with the religious Nation of Islam the view that racism would not end until black people had a land of their own, which was separate and independent. Malcolm X was later to break with the Nation of Islam, which he found too extreme (and also corrupt). He went on to steer into being the Organization of Afro-American Unity. Malcolm X's new position (just prior to his assassination) is summed up by activist Shawna Maglangbayan: "It was one in which he advocated a struggle for the fulfilment of the black man's human rights in the United States with national independence in mind as the ultimate outcome. In other words: 'Let's struggle to build an independent nation right where we are by initiating a struggle towards the fulfilment of our immediate and most basic needs and the progressive establishment of our own separate institutions in every field.' Malcolm X's objective, his goal, the very essence of his OAAU's unmistakably national separatist program, was to achieve national-racial-autonomy as a first step in a long and complicated process of struggle which would eventually culminate in independent black nationhood."

In many ways Malcolm X moves the ideas of Garvey further; he is more concerned with political action now, with the immediate realities and hardships of black people. Shawna Maglangbayan argues: "The fact is that post-slavery national separatists in the USA had never concentrated on political action. Booker T. Washington's national-separatist program omitted any emphasis on political activity; it subordinated everything to the goal of economic self-sufficiency and technological advancement. Garvey's UNIA in America was involved in no political action of significance. The same holds true for Elijah Muhammad's Nation of Islam (they just hated white folks).'' She argues that Malcolm X was the first national separatist in the United States to realise that without a political dimension ''a vacuum was created which has been filled by the reactionary, integrationist, boot-licking stratum of America.'' Historian Robert Hill says: ''Indeed the disintegration of the UNIA as a radical political force began the moment Garvey resorted to the ideology of racial purity.''

The difference was that Malcolm X took Garveyism one, or maybe one thousand steps further by making it clear that it is all very well and good being separate and developing the homeland, but with no vote, bad housing and poor education, a political programme was needed there and then in order to develop a secure future. To be fair on Garvey, after his deportation to Jamaica he became intensely politically active even forming his own party. However, in America, he was not a significant political force. It took the son of a Garveyite to fill the gap.

The connections between the teachings of Marcus Garvey and the philosophies of Elijah Muhammad and Malcolm X are clearly strong. In a letter to the *Jamaica Gleaner*, November 17th, 1964, Thomas Harvey, President General of the UNIA pointed to Garvey's influence: ''Garvey paved the way for all local leaders who have emerged since his death. Most of them were his understudies or followers who were inspired by his dynamic leadership, and the universality of his appeal for justice, equality and independence for the Negro peoples throughout the world.''

In 1964 the *Jamaica Gleaner* ran what was to be one of the last interviews with Malcolm X, just prior to him tragically being gunned down at a meeting in New York on February 21st of that year. He was asked how much was he influenced, as a thinking black man, by his West Indian mother. He said: ''Well, it probably did...Historians have written the fact that slaves were never brought directly from Africa to America, but rather they were first taken to the West Indies or Caribbean area, where there were special persons whose job it was to break the will of the slave. Once his will was broken, his language and cultural characteristics were destroyed, then he was brought to America. So that the black people or the Africans who remained in the Caribbean area, their will was never broken as thoroughly as the will of those Africans who ultimately ended up on these shores.'' He goes on to make what must be an over-generous analysis of the Caribbean (particularly Jamaica), but the sentiment is correct: ''Most West Indians, most people in the Caribbean area, are still proud that they are black, proud of the African blood, and their heritage; and I think this type of pride was instilled in my mother, and she instilled it in us, too, to the best degree she could. She had — despite the fact that her father was white — more African leanings, and African pride and a desire to be identified with Africa. In fact she was an active member of the Marcus Garvey movement.''

Malcolm X also noted that the American Black Muslim movement generally must look to Garvey as its greatest inspirer. ''Every time you see another nation on the African continent become independent, you know that Marcus Garvey is alive. It was Marcus Garvey's philosophy of Pan-Africanism that initiated the entire freedom movement, which brought about the independence of African nations. And had it not been for Marcus Garvey, and the foundations laid by him, you would find no independent nations in the Caribbean today... All the freedom movements that are taking place right here in America today were initiated by the work and teachings of Marcus Garvey. The entire Black Muslim philosophy here in America is feeding upon the seeds that were planted by Marcus Garvey.''

The 1980s have witnessed the emergence of another popular Black Muslim

Fiery speech: Garvey-inspired Louis Farrakhan, the leader of the Nation of Islam, delivers his speech to 25,000 people at Madison Square Garden. Farrakhan urged the over-whelmingly black audience to take control of their own destiny.

leader, Louis Farrakhan. It is clear that this Muslim leader developed his style and many of his ideas from Marcus Garvey. Like Garvey, there is no tolerance for a view of God that allows oppression and self-hatred. Farrakhan's speeches expand a Garvey belief that you cannot love your neighbour as yourself without first liking yourself and knowing who you are. Throughout his life Garvey had remained impatient with what he saw as the restrictions of traditional black religion. Garvey makes this point when he says: "Man is able to shape his own character, direct his own life and shape his own ends. When God breathed into the nostrils of man the breath of life, and bestowed upon him the authority of 'Lord of Creation', he never intended that the individual should descend to the level of a serf or a slave, but that he should be always man, in the fullest possession of his sense and with the truest knowledge of himself." Garvey is saying to black people, that their failings in the past, present and future, is a failure not to know truly who they are. It is at the same time a historical and mystical analysis: the sin of the 'Negro' was that he failed to know himself. The sin of the white race was that it moved away from the true function of man and enslaved another — instead of being a caretaker of creation. Garvey was convinced that this state of affairs would ultimately lead to the destruction of the whole of humanity unless a way out was found for the black race.

He says emphatically: "Remember that you are men, that God created you Lords of this creation. Lift up yourselves, take yourselves out of the mire and hitch your hopes to the stars; Yes, rise as high as the very stars themselves. Let no man pull you down, Let no man destroy your ambition; because man is but your companion, your equal, man is your brother, he is not your Lord, He is not your sovereign master."

Garvey thus managed to combine the practical and the mystical in order to further his doctrine of 'success'. This can be seen in the following recollection by an original Charter member of the Toronto UNIA. He says: "Garvey even went as far as to say Black people should have a religion of their own, a God of their own, a Black God, because when you worship someone else who doesn't look like you, then you are in trouble. And I agree with that, I really do. To me, a humble black fellow in the street, Garvey gave me a real bit of hope. He said get brains, get learning, go to school and learn."

For Farrakhan, also, this essential message of black success is central to his thinking and not, indeed, without impact. In September 1984, he had become so popular that he attracted 25,000 people to New York City's Madison Square Garden — a place where years before Garvey himself had enthralled one of his biggest audiences.

Farrakhan's ideas provoked sharp exchanges over black-Jewish relations — Edward Koch, the Jewish major of New York City denounced him as a 'Nazi in clerical garb'. Farrakhan declared, to his 25,000 Madison Square audience, that he, like Garvey before him, was being hounded by the press and politicians: "I've been called a deceiver, a Hitler lover, the new Hitler, a Klan lover, a con-man. They even called me the devil himself. Mr Koch said I should burn in hell. Well, all I can say to that is that in New York City black people live in hell. And if you're the gatekeeper of hell, then you must be the devil himself."

This Muslim leader first entered black political life a quarter of a century ago as the young protégé of Malcolm X. They were both in the Nation of Islam. Farrakhan was named the minister of the Black Muslim's Boston mosque and he acquired a substantial following, even among black militants and working people who had no relationship with the Nation of Islam. In 1964, Malcolm broke from the Nation of Islam and became 'political' — Farrakhan, however, remained loyal to the group and his conservative mentor, the aged Elijah Muhammad.

After Elijah Muhammad's death in 1975, the Nation of Islam was radically transformed by its new leader, Wallace D. Muhammad. The sect's anti-white dogmas were summarily dropped and the theological basis of the organisation was made to conform closely to orthodox Sunni Islam. Farrakhan broke from the reformed group in 1978 and in January 1981 announced the rebirth of the 'Nation of Islam' under his leadership.

In a speech made in Jamaica in 1985, Farrakhan, an American with a Jamaican father, talked of the inspiration of Garvey: "Mr Garvey came from Jamaica to America and there amongst your black brothers, he made a tremendous impact. When I was a little boy of 11 years old, I went to my uncle's home and I saw the picture there of a black man on the wall. That was very strange, because in those days we never had pictures of black people on any wall. It was King George, Queen Victoria or a false representation of Jesus. So when I saw this blackman,

Marcus Garvey advocate of black self-reliance.

I said to my uncle 'Who is that man?' And my uncle said 'that is a man who has come to unite all black people'. I immediately loved him because, as a little boy, I used to wonder about the justice of God. If God would send a Moses to deliver Israel why, he would surely send a deliverer for you and me. I knew this was the man, so I stood on a chair to drink in his features and I asked my uncle where is this man so that I can meet him and join him. My uncle looked at me and said he was dead. Tears began to run down my cheeks — for I felt I had come so close to the deliverer and he was gone. Little did I know that one day I would return to the island that gave birth to Marcus Garvey and my father, with a message of hope and deliverance based on all the great masters — there is nothing new under the sun."

Farrakhan, like his mentor Garvey, and to a certain extent Malcolm X, made his impact through his remarkable gift of oratory. Other links with Garvey are to be found in his message of self-reliance, the overcoming of self-hatred and in the need for the pursuit of black economic success. While Garvey often used a Christian framework to ground his ideas, Farrakhan does the same with Islam. The bitterness however, which Garvey felt toward white Christianity is eloquently summed up in a *Negro World* editorial which he wrote in 1923: "The Negro is now accepting the religion of the real Christ, not the property-robbing, gold-stealing, diamond-exploiting Christ, but the Christ of Love, Justice and Mercy. The Negro wants no more of the white man's religion as it applies to his race, for it is a lie and a face; it is a propaganda pure and simple to make fools of a race and rob the precious world, the gift of God to man."

The essence of Farrakhan's economic message is profoundly Garveyite, based on his perception of God and his relationship to his people. The God of the UNIA and the God of Farrakhan's organisation differs from a notion of a God who has already 'cooked the books' so all you have to do is sit and wait. Garvey and Farrakhan's God is a God of self-reliance. "There is no way" Farrakhan says, "Jamaica could be in the condition that it is in if religion was in the right state. There is no way that the masses of Jamaica could be instilled with a self-defeating inferiority complex, hating the blackness of their skin, hating their origin in the world, bending and bowing to things that are white and looking down upon everything that is black." He goes on: "God does not want you to hate the way he created you, for you cannot love him and hate yourself and if you love God you must love the way he created you as a blackman. Jesus said as a man thinketh so is he. How does Jamaica think? Jamaica has been beaten down over the years, free and ignorant at the same time — ignorance is an enslaving power. God is the best knower — the knowledge of God is like being in the sun — you can't be in darkness at the same time. Therefore if you are ignorant and say you know God then you are a liar. We must be people who want knowledge — because this is what separates man and woman from the lower animals. You are not an animal, you were created to master the universe, but Jamaica suffers from nearly 40 per cent functional illiteracy. Something is being contrived to keep Jamaica under the foot of imperialism. Jamaica must rise as a free people but you can never rise on ignorance; hating yourself, you cannot rise, looking to the white man to do for you what you can get up and do for yourself."

Like Garvey before him, Farrakhan's thinking holds appeal not only for the poor people but for the black middle-class as well, whose upward mobility in the public sector had been checked by a shrinking in Federal Government social programmes and a less than committed approach to affirmative action. To disgruntled black businessmen also, Farrakhan's philosophy for action provides a simplistic, yet historically popular solution.

The Nation of Islam created an economic network termed POWER — People Organised and Working for Economic Rebirth. Essentially a strategy to promote black petty capitalism, POWER projected a system of co-operation between black-owned firms which sell to black consumers.

What is significant about POWER is its kinship to earlier black 'self-help' programmes. During the nineteenth century, conservative black educator Booker T. Washington launched the National Negro Business League, a coalition of black entrepreneurs, which promoted the development of all-black insurance firms, funeral homes, groceries and retail establishments. A generation later, in the 1920s, Marcus Garvey created the Negro Factories Corporation, a group of black businessmen who attempted to seize control of the black consumer market.

Malcolm X and Louis Farrakhan can be described as the prominent male offspring of the Garvey fatherhood. However, the unsung heroism of women in the Garvey movement was pervasive, despite Garvey's own backward ideas on women: "Colored women there is a better place for you in the world, a place of honor in the black man's palace in Africa. To decorate the legislative palaces in Africa." Ironically, Amy Ashwood and Amy Jacques Garvey played critical roles in the preservation of the Garvey legacy. Amy Ashwood, co-founder of the UNIA, went on to be a prominent member of the Pan-African movement, while Amy Jacques single-handedly published the most widely read collection of writings by Marcus Garvey, 'The Philosophy and Opinions of Marcus Garvey vol 1 and 2.'

Sister Mariamne Samad, born at the height of the Garvey movement in New York, with Garveyite parents, was a Garvey child.

Other women took up the Garvey heritage and in their own ways continued to keep the Garvey message alive. Sister Mariamne Samad was born into a Garveyite family in America—her father was Guyanese, her mother, American. After extensive travels in Africa in the 1960s and 1970s, she settled in Jamaica in 1976 with her Jamaican husband Abdul who was in Garvey's African Legion.

She remembers a different childhood to other children: "We wore a uniform. Not to school, of course, but in the afternoons, when the other children were out playing in the streets, we were off to the Garvey Club in Harlem. The uniform for the very young was black socks, black shoes, then when you were Miss Teenage — you wore black stockings, with a green shirt, red tie and a cap; it was so cute, we were always marching, ready for battle. You didn't even want to be like other children. It was a strange life and, I have discovered too a lonely life."

One of the important things which Sister Samad cherished was her black doll: "Yes, we had black dolls. I remember my first doll was bigger than me, because they made these huge dolls and my godfather wanted to give me a present, so he didn't buy one of the little ones, he thought I would grow up with the doll, you know. In fact I did have her until 1937."

She claims that much of the work that she did in the 1950s as a woman, re-emerged with the black youngsters of the sixties, followers of Black Power. She said: "In the 1950s I formed the Sankori Nubian Cultural Workshop. We did fashion shows, we started African fashions as fashions. There are a lot of things that are being called African fashions in today's world, even worn by Africans, that were actually started in Harlem because we took the African clothing that we saw and we stylised it; we started the abbuba for the women and I created the dashiki for the men in 1958. It was like giving royalty to the black man. I began to do weddings of people in the community, African-Americanised outfits. We propagated the story of Shaka, we wanted everyone who was black to know about Shaka."

****

The son of Marcus Garvey, Marcus Garvey Jr, argued that his father was one of the foundation stones of the Black Power movement that gripped America and Jamaica during the 1960s. He quoted his father: "Power is the only argument that satisfies man. Except the individual, the race or the nation has power that is exclusive, it means that that individual race or nation will be bound by the will of the other who possesses this great qualification...Hence it is advisable for the Negro to get power of every kind. Power in education, science, industry, politics and higher government. That kind of power, that will stand out signally, so that other races and nations can see and if they will not see, feel."

Although Garvey is without question the father of Black Power in Jamaica, some critics have argued that it would be wrong merely to reduce the Black Power movement in America to the influence of Garvey. The argument goes that when the UNIA finally collapsed in America, the energy for Black Nationalism was incubated in the black ghettoes until, in the 1960s, it leapt beyond the ghetto into what was to become an ideological reaction to the bankruptcy of liberalism and civil rights control. It had to do with cultural assumptions that knew nothing of Garvey — they were part of a reaction to the specific liberal institutions in America that were seen to be unable to deliver, with their worst hypocrisy culminating in the Vietnam

Opposite page:
Panther Power: Marcus Garvey's writing was on the shortlist of many Black Panther activists.

war. Therefore the 1960s and the Black Power movement is seen to have had a dynamic of its own over and above the inspiration of Garvey; although true, what cannot be denied however, is the symbolic significance of Garvey during the 1960s Black Power upsurge, with many of the demands put forward by the Black Power movement having been articulated by Garvey years before.

Black power represented a new slant to the old debate — the new slogan made a nationalist appeal without employing the strict religious fundamentalism, seen for example in the Black Muslims, which had tended to alienate intellectuals and the young cynics who dwelt in the ghetto. Secondly, the Black Power movement, unlike earlier nationalist movements, ignored the question of land, whether of the back-to-Africa or five-States-in-the-South variety. Thus, it avoided becoming involved in endless and diversionary detours over how to get back to Africa or which States were suitable. Instead, it focused the attention of militants on the problem of how to achieve power where black people were actually living, here and now.

The attraction to the Black Power movement came with an assertion of black self-worth and identity. There was the recognition also that the civil rights movement was intended to benefit the middle-class blacks, and that integration meant assimilation into white society and the submergence of whatever separate black culture existed. For the frustrated and rebellious ghetto youth, Black Power was at once an energy of hope in the midst of gloom. Kwame Ture, then the chairman of the Student Non-violent Co-ordinating Committee (SNCC), wrote in the spring of 1967 that the Black Power movement "could speak to the growing militancy of young people in the urban ghetto."

Unable to come through with the material advancement or moral uplift it promised, the non-violent civil rights movement became discredited, with young black activists attacking its paternalistic aspects. They turned inward and began talking of race pride, black consciousness, black history and culture. In short, they laid the basis for the cultural nationalism which has become the characteristic of the Black Power movement. Imprisoned Black Panther leader Huey P. Newton said in March 1967: "We believe that it's important for us to recognise our origins and to identify with the revolutionary black people of Africa and people of colour throughout the world. But as far as returning, per se, to the ancient customs, we don't see any necessity in this. And also, we say that the only culture that is worth holding on to is revolutionary culture, for change, for the better."

Black Power, as originally articulated by the SNCC in 1966, was anti-racist. It attacked white paternalism, but urged whites to go into their own communities to work against institutionalised racism while black activists organised in black communities to assault the same enemy. But white activists, by and large, moved into anti-war action instead of attacking domestic racism, thus occasioning bitter attacks by black militants against the white left. Norman Mailer, in his excellent book 'Cannibals and Christians', describes how the white left's diversion to Vietnam helped crush a black revolution and save President Lyndon Johnson from his own hypocrisy, he said: "So the civil rights movement was going to crowd everything else out of the newspapers. There was going to be no way to control the Negro Movement, and no way to convince the Negro Movement that their victory was due to his particular attentions. You can never convince a movement of your power unless you can send them back after you have called them forth. So the President needed another issue. Then it came to the President. Hot damn. Vietnam. Vietnam, that little old country which had been under his nose all these years. Things were getting too quiet in Vietnam. If there was one thing hotter

Huey P. Newton: Major Black Panther spokesman.

than Harlem in the summer, it was air raids on rice paddies and napalm on red gooks. Now he had a game. When the war got too good, and everybody was giving too much space to that, he could always tell the Nigras it was good time to be marching on the White House. When they got a little too serious he could bring back Vietnam.''

   Jim Forman, head of the SNCC's international affairs commission and movement strategist and theoretician, offered an explanation of the Black Power orientation: ''Not surprisingly accusations of 'extremism' and 'racism in reverse' filled the air. Those accusations reflected the fact that the slogan 'Black Power' was frightening to white Americans in general and the US Government in particular because of its revolutionary implications. That Government knows that whites have power and blacks do not. Therefore, the idea of poor black people, especially in the cities of the United States, uniting for power on the basis of independent political action — and against the foreign wars of the United States — represented a type of revolution.''

By the time of the Newark Black Power Conference in July 1967, it was clear that black power meant different things to different people, and the divisions in the political groupings within Black Power became manifest at that historic meeting. Moving from the political right to left, one could distinguish five categories, each of them with an element of Garveyism. As one old American Garveyite told me: "It was really weird, we were just doing our thing working away at the Garvey cause, then all of a sudden these youngsters got up and shouted Black Power, and I said to myself hang on we've been saying this for years."

The first category is Black Power as black capitalism. This was espoused, for example, by the nationalist Black Muslims who urged blacks to set up businesses, factories and independent farming operations. Even Richard Nixon, at that time Presidential aspirant, in a speech in 1968 called for a move away from massive government financed social welfare programmes to "more black ownership, black pride, black jobs... black power in the most constructive sense. Black militants," according to Nixon, should seek to become capitalists — "to have a share of the wealth."

The second group saw the overriding need for more black politicians. A leading exponent was Amiri Baraka, well known nationalist and author of the play'Dutchman'. In 1968 he was a member of the United Brothers, Newark's black united front, which sought control of the city and were active in cooling out the riots which developed after the murder of Rev Martin Luther King Jr. Baraka believed that control could be won through the ballot. He believed in the need to work with others including the police, in attempting to find peaceful solutions to black people's struggles. He even met with right wing organisations such as 'Imperiale'. In an interview with the *Washington Post* he said: "Our aim is to bring about black self-government in Newark by 1970." Baraka went on, "We have a membership that embraces every social area in Newark. It is a wide cross-section of business, professional and political life." He continues: "I'm in favour of black people taking power by the quickest, easiest, most successful means they can employ. Malcolm X said the ballot or the bullet. Newark is a particular situation where the ballot seems to be advantageous. I believe we have to survive. I didn't invent the white man. What we're trying to do is deal with him in the best way we can... Black men are not murderers... What we don't want to be are die-ers." Baraka added that he had "more respect for Imperiale, because he doesn't lie, like white liberals." Imperiale, he said, "had the mistaken understanding that we wanted to come up to his territory and do something. That was the basic clarification. We don't want to be bothered and I'm sure he doesn't want to be bothered." This is almost identical to the reasons Garvey gave for his controversial meetings with the Ku Klux Klan.

Another Black Power leader from Newark, Nathan Wright, was the chief proponent of the third strand of Black Power — group integration. In his book, 'Black Power and Urban Unrest', Wright urges black people to band together as a group to seek entry into the American mainstream. For example, he called for organised efforts by blacks "to seek executive positions in corporations, bishoprics, deanships of cathedrals, superintendencies of schools and high management positions in banks, stores, investment houses, legal firms, civic and government agencies and factories." Wright's position differs from black capitalism or integration politics in that he calls for an organised group effort, instead of individual effort, to win entry into the American system.

The political centre of the black power spectrum, however, and the most widely accepted formulation was Black Power as black control of the black communities.

Martin Luther King went to Jamaica in June 1965. He felt a sense of freedom which he had never felt in America.

This is what the SNCC originally meant by the term. Floyd McKissik, who was national director of the Congress of Racial Equality, put it thus: "The program is to seek control of the education system, the political-economic system and the administration of our own communities. We must control our own courts and our own police... Ownership of businesses in the ghetto must be transferred to black people — either individually or collectively." In short, black control of the black community had slowly been transformed into black elite control of the black community, which began to be a buttress in order for the white establishment to have control over the ghettoes through co-option — this needed to be changed.

If the latter formulation formed the political centre of Black Power the most 'popular' and widely published tenet was the push for Black Liberation as envisaged by the Black Panthers. The inability of the white left to seriously deal with racism and repression accelerated the process towards black militancy. Kwame Ture, under these conflicting pressures, announced that whites "are the enemy or at best, irrelevant." He organised black united fronts, whose unity consisted in shared blackness and concern for survival. Survival quickly became the uppermost concern. Socialism became irrelevant for Ture because he foresaw a race war: black against white. He did not anticipate any class struggle in the ortho-dox sense, hence class analysis was rendered useless. To Ture all blacks formed one class: the hunted. All whites formed another class: the hunters and their accomplices.

He believed that blacks would eventually win the projected race war, although there was concern at the increasing number of deaths of black militants and the possibility of genocide and extermination, Martin Luther King's assassination adding new weight to this concern.

Shortly after King's death and only a few hours before he was jailed, Eldridge Cleaver, minister of information of the Black Panthers, said: ''The death of Dr King signals the end of an era and the beginning of a terrible and bloody chapter that may remain unwritten, because there may be no scribe left to capture on paper the holocaust to come.''

Earlier Cleaver had expressed a widespread view when he wrote in the May issue of *Ramparts*: ''If the white mother country is to have victory over the black colony, it is the duty of black revolutionaries to ensure that the imperialists receive no more than a pyrrhic victory, written in the blood of what America might have become.''

Kwame Ture was born in Port of Spain, Trinidad. He was 11 when he and his family emigrated to Harlem, New York. He married South African singer Miriam Makeba in April 1968 with whom he went to live in West Africa. At the time, Ture resigned from the Panther Party, saying that he could no longer support ''the present tactics and methods which the party is using to coerce and force everyone to submit to its authority.'' Ture returned to the United States in March 1970, and he became involved in ''a relentless struggle against the poison of drugs

Tommie Smith (centre) and John Carlos give the Black Power salute during the 1968 Olympics. They also wear black socks the symbol of black poverty.

Martyrs and militants, Black Panther mourners at the funeral of Jonathan Jackson brother of Black Panther leader, George Jackson. Garvey was used as a symbolic inspiration as they began the Cultural revolution of the Sixties in America.

Watts Los Angeles 1965, it was a long hot summer — these men are not dead but have been arrested on suspicion of looting. Watts was to see intense rioting with many deaths and massive damage to property.

in the black community." Some have argued that drugs were a fundamental factor in the collapse of the Black Power movement in America.

If any concessions were won by the Black Power movement it was not through an overflowing of generosity on the part of the white government. It had more to do with white America's preoccupation with her international face. How could she be christian abroad and cannibal at home, especially in the light of the propaganda war being waged against Communism? Norman Mailer sums it up well: "We have even had a Negro Revolution in which we did not believe. We have had it, yes we have had it, because we could not afford to lose votes in Africa and India, South America, Vietnam, the Philippines, name any impoverished place: we have been running in a world election against the collective image of the Russians, and so we have had to give the black man his civil rights or Africa was so much nearer to Marx. But there has not been much like love in the civil rights. We have never been too authentic. No." This is precisely in line with Garvey's emphasis on the freedom and unity of Africa. This was how Garvey perceived Black Nationalism — working from a strong continental base.

Walter Rodney, black academic and political visionary, who was killed in Guyana in 1980, commented on Garvey's inspiration to the Black Power movement thus: "Marcus Garvey was one of the first advocates of Black Power, and is still today the greatest spokesman ever to have been produced by the movement of black consciousness. 'A race without power and authority is a race without respect', wrote Garvey. He spoke to all Africans on the earth, whether they lived in Africa, South America, the West Indies or North America, and he made blacks aware of their strength when united." He goes on: "The USA was his main field of operation, after he had been chased out of Jamaica by the sort of people who today pretend to have made him a hero. All of the black leaders who have advanced the cause in the USA since Garvey's time have recognised the international nature of the struggle against White Power."

****

Garvey's plan for a united and independent Africa needed the support of Africa itself; sadly the colonialist policy of divide and rule often left African nations divided and the idea of a wider unity seemed to be a dream. Two leaders, however, who would subsequently have tragic ends, attempted to build on this Garveyite hope: Kwame Nkrumah of Ghana and Patrice Lumumba of the Congo.

It was the historian C.L.R. James who is credited with giving the young Nkrumah the right connections in order for him to begin his historic work. James says: "I met him first in New York in about 1941. He saw a great deal of my friends and political associates, and we became very intimately associated. Then in 1943, he said he was going to England to study law, whereupon I wrote a letter to George Padmore." He goes on: "This letter said that Nkrumah, a young African, was coming to live in England. I said that he was not very bright but that he was determined to throw the imperialists out of Africa. I asked Padmore to see him and do his best for him, in other words, educate him politically as much as possible." Nkrumah, it transpired, was a brilliant student and he was to give Padmore's London based organisation fresh vitality and purpose.

Nkrumah soon got his biggest break when a group of middle-class Africans on the Gold Coast formed a political organisation called the Convention Party. They wanted an end to colonial rule so that the black man could rule in his own country. Hearing of this young like-minded African in London, they sent for Nkrumah to join them and fight for independence. He wasted no time in organising the Youth Party. Such was his popularity that, in a short time, he had won the support of the majority of those in the Convention Party and, in fact, went on to form his own organisation, the Convention People's Party. The middle-class leaders that Nkrumah usurped were vexed, as he had roundly condemned them for being stooges of the British government. A bitter row ensued. Nkrumah went on to win independence for Ghana having conquered the middle-class. Nkrumah, like Garvey, did not hang around for the British to finish their picnic. He wanted self-government and he wanted it now. His philosophy was 'positive action'; he managed to mobilise the vast masses of the people of Ghana against the British Colonial Government. As C.L.R. James says: "Nobody in Africa has hurled a whole population at an imperialist government." Nkrumah and the main leaders were inevitably thrown in jail once they became a real threat to the colonial rulers. But Nkrumah cleverly masterminded leadership from his cell and his party won the elections in an overwhelming victory. While the British contemplated sending in the Army, they feared that this would precipitate the break-up of the Commonwealth and so, reluctantly, with little choice, relinquished power in Ghana.

Kwame Nkrumah helped to turn Ghana into a model nation. He said that whenever he thought of African freedom, only one name came up and that was Marcus Garvey.

Sadly Nkrumah made the mistake of waiting until 1957 before he declared independence when it could have been his in 1951. This was to prove disastrous and one of the causes of his later tragic fall. Nkrumah followed Nehru and declared Ghana a republic, setting a pattern since followed by nearly all the African states and inspired by Marcus Garvey. Such was the impression of Garvey in the mind of Nkrumah that he named his country's national shipping company the Black Star Line.

Nkrumah then sent for George Padmore to organise the first International Conference of African Independent States. He also organised the first conference for African freedom fighters. With Nkrumah's declaration of a desire for a united Africa, African unity was on the move — a united Africa being the one and only way to fight the colonial threat.

In Nkrumah's address to the 15th session of the General Assembly of the United Nations, September 23rd, 1960 he stated: "For years and years Africa has been the foot-stool of colonialism and imperialism, exploitation and degradation. From the north to south, from east to west, her sons languished in the chains of slavery and humiliation, and Africa's exploiters and self-appointed controllers of her destiny strode across our land with incredible inhumanity, without mercy, without shame, and without honour. Those days are gone and gone forever, and now I, an African, stand before this august Assembly of the United Nations and speak with a voice of peace and freedom, proclaiming to the world the dawn of a new era."

When Garvey proclaimed in 1916 the slogan of Garveyism: "Africa for the Africans, at home and abroad," there were only two independent nations in Africa, but the year 1960 was a year of fulfilment when 28 nations emerged from colonial rule. Nkrumah, in another address, this time in 1958 in Accra, to an All-African Conference speaking on the legacy that Marcus Garvey had left for African freedom, said: "It has warmed us that so many of our brothers from across the seas are with us. We take their presence here as a manifestation of the keen interest in our struggle for a free Africa. We must never forget that they are a part of us.

"These sons and daughters of Africa were taken away from our shores and, despite all the centuries which have separated us, they have not forgotten their ancestral links. Many of them made no small contribution to the cause of African

A happy scene at the farewell ball in the State House, Accra, The Queen and President Nkrumah enjoy a joke. However, Britain now had to deal seriously with African people who wanted to determine their own lives.

freedom. A name that springs immediately to mind in this connection is Marcus Garvey. Long before many of us were even conscious of our own degradation Marcus Garvey fought for African national and racial equality.''

The story of Nkrumah's fall proved a forerunner for the fate of many other African leaders that followed. Apart from wasting money on such things as buying planes and warships, trappings rather than infrastructure, he was also too crude in his philosophy for a United Africa — it became more rhetorical than practical. The masses suffered heavy taxation and when the price of cocoa dropped considerably on the world market, Ghana went bankrupt. Nkrumah began to amass power to himself and the dream was over. However, as C.L.R. James, says: "Nkrumah's failure was not a failure of individual personality. It was the impossibility of establishing a viable regime and bringing some order into the messes that the imperialists had left behind. Second, what is astonishing is not the failures but the successes. When did so many millions move so far and so fast? To Africans, and people of African descent everywhere, the name of Nkrumah became for many years a symbol of release from the subordination to which they had been subjected for so many centuries. After Marcus Garvey, there is no other name that is so symbolical of African freedom as the name of Nkrumah."

Among those invited to Nkrumah's meeting for African freedom fighters, was the man from the Congo, Patrice Lumumba. The Congo was brutally exploited by the French and Belgians all seeking those precious sticks of ivory. Patrice Lumumba was Congo's first Prime Minister but his reign only lasted three months.

He subsequently met a violent death after months in prison. The late Fifties had seen pressure building in those countries without independence. Plans were made by the British and French to get on with the process of decolonisation. In the case of the Congo, the Belgian authorities were initially pleased that Lumumba emerged as leader of the new state. After all, he had given lavish praise for the Belgian work of 'civilising' Africa. On June 30th 1960, Independence Day, Lumumba revealed that really he was a closet Garveyite. On that day, the Belgians had not planned for Lumumba to make any speech whatsoever. He suddenly rose to his feet, grabbed the microphone and told his people that the colonisation of the Congo was "nothing other than the domination of the whites over the blacks." He demystified the colonisation he had himself once termed a "work of civilization".

He went on to say; "We have suffered humiliating slavery which was imposed on us by force. Let us show the world what the black man can do when he works in freedom!" In a single powerful statement Lumumba had resurrected Garvey, in other words he made mockery of this so called granting of independence and explained to his people what African independence really meant. The Belgian colonialists looked on red-faced as 'their man' turned against them.

Not even a day had passed after Lumumba's speech, when fear swept the European settlers at the realisation that the black man might really want to rule himself. Belgian troops (which had never left the Congo) were mobilised and they went on a rampage of slaughter. Tribal warfare also emerged, manipulated in a policy of divide and rule. The country was thrown into chaos and Lumumba began to sense the last act of this tragedy. He suffered from desertions in his ranks and it became evident that he lacked a class of people around him who were committed to the accomplishment of a free, independent and united Africa. He also suffered from opportunists, who saw the collapse of the country as an opportunity to gain a foothold in provinces which would then secede from the state.

Lumumba was betrayed by one after another of those in his government; he was confronted with Belgian inspired opposition within the ranks of the Congolese army and faced with the aggression of 10,000 Belgian soldiers as well as the secessionists forces helped by mercenaries from South Africa. Lumumba had even called in the United Nations troops, who then proved to be hostile to his leadership. Even the great Nkrumah had let him down, his 3,000 soldiers teaming up with the British became more concerned with disarming Lumumba forces than giving the Belgians a good hiding.

The stage was set for the final act. It came on September 14th, 1960, when Joseph Mobutu staged a coup. Lumumba had been Prime Minister for less than three months when he was placed under house arrest by Mobutu and his forces. Lumumba managed to escape but was soon captured and turned over to the Belgians. He wrote his last letter, addressed to his wife, Pauline, which was to become his last political statement: "All through my struggle for the independence of my country, I have never doubted for a single instant the final triumph of the sacred cause to which my companions and I have devoted all our lives... Dead or alive, free or in prison... it is not myself who counts. It is the Congo, it is our poor people for whom independence has been transformed into a cage... I know and feel in my heart that sooner or later my people will rid themselves of all their enemies, both internal and external, and that they will rise as one man to say 'No' to the degradation and shame of colonialism, and regain their dignity in the clear light of the sun. Without dignity there is no liberty, without justice there is no dignity, and without independence there are no free men.

"Neither brutality, nor cruelty nor torture will ever bring me to ask for mercy, for I prefer to die with my head unbowed, my faith unshakable and with profound trust in the destiny of my country, rather than live under subjection and disregarding sacred principles. History will one day have its say, but it will not be the history that is taught in Brussels, Paris, Washington or in the United Nations... Africa will write her own history, and it will be a glorious and dignified history."

On January 17th, 1961, Patrice Lumumba was killed after a month and a half of intense and savage torture.

The activist, Shawna Maglangbayan, draws the links between the vision of Lumumba and that of Garvey: "As was with Garvey, Patrice Lumumba was unable to accomplish the high task he had set before himself: the establishment in the Congo of a black economic, political, cultural, industrial, scientific and military bastion for the liberation of Africa and the rest of the black world. It was to this end that he mobilized the national-separatist aspirations of the black masses in the Congo. It was toward the accomplishment of this goal that he sacrificed himself."

Lumumba knew that the Congo was strategically an excellent place from which one could base the development of a black military state to fight for a United Africa. No leader emerging from colonialism was ever so swiftly and brutally destroyed — clearly the vision of a United Africa developing into a tangible power base, was an African dream but a European nightmare.

Nkrumah and Lumumba were not the only two influenced by the Garvey vision: The East African leader, Jomo Kenyatta, had come under the influence of Garveyism in London, when he, along with George Padmore, began to develop the idea of Pan-Africanism. George Padmore writing in the *Jamaica Gleaner* of 1954 on Jomo Kenyatta says, 'Kenyatta was repeatedly spurned by the Colonial Office, and the Communists invited him to visit Moscow in 1939, but he returned to England when he refused to let African nationalism be exploited for Russian foreign policies. Kenyatta met Marcus Garvey and became converted to the philosophy 'Africa for Africans' and after Garvey's death, Kenyatta and other Africans and West Indians formed the Pan-African Federation. A Congress in Manchester, England was called in 1945 to plan a broad strategy of African liberation.

"Kenyatta returned to Kenya in 1946 to assume leadership of the African Union. Within one year over 100,000 members were enrolled. In the following year Nkrumah returned to the Gold Coast to lead West African nationalists. Other Pan-African leaders returned to South and Central Africa to organise political parties, trade unions and co-operatives."

Jomo Kenyatta. Father of Kenyan independence. A great admirer of Garvey he considered himself an active member of the UNIA.

Kenyatta was to say on many occasions that as a young man he met Marcus Garvey in London, had heard Garvey speak several times in Hyde Park and considered himself to be a fully fledged member of UNIA.

Patrice Lumumba with a message that was not expected, the spirit of Garvey certainly stirred that day.

Humiliation: Patrice Lumumba was sentenced for inciting riots in Stanleyville. They escort him barefooted to his prison cell. He died later of brutal injuries.

JAMAICAN HERO

Garvey returned to Jamaica in November 1927 after two years and nine months in Atlanta Federal Prison. Garvey was now 40, but still young; he had managed to develop a mass movement within ten years. Martin Luther King, Jr, was later to say that Garvey's true place in history was due to the fact that he was "the first man, on a mass scale, to give millions of Negroes a sense of dignity and destiny."

As Garvey stood at the quayside in Kingston, there was reported to be the largest crowd ever assembled in the Kingston area. It was as if all of Jamaica's one million population had turned out to get a glimpse of his return. An account of his arrival was given to me by Garvey's friend, J.P. Vivian Durham. He said: "In the notorious trial of Marcus Garvey in the United States the man hadn't the chance of a dog, in the light of the prosecuting attorney's emotive and gallingly unfair, prejudiced and offensive outburst to the jury (which in those days could have included members of the nefarious Ku Klux Klan) — 'Members of the jury, shall we let the tiger loose?'

"So Garvey was convicted and in his own words here in Jamaica, 'handcuffed and dragged across the streets of Harlem like a common thief'.

"Like many which comprised the Jerusalem rabble decades before, perjured witnesses were cajoled to sell their soul for a mess of pottage paying tribute to the throne of Annanias. The green eyed monster 'jealousy' had an unbridled and free passage through traitor's gate — the object was to obtain a conviction at any cost. Coming back to Garvey's welcome home from 'The Tomb' (name of the prison in Atlanta), it was a thrilling and exciting spectacle to see men, women and children in their thousands assembled from early morning to wait the arrival of the ship at 2pm on that historic Saturday afternoon.

"Members of the local UNIA comprising Black Cross nurses, Scouts, Girl Guides, labourers, handcart operators, rich and poor. The ship docked on time, and, there, amidst the roaring of applause of those within and without the pier, emerged Marcus Garvey attired in a grey flannel suit, brown shoes and a Jippi Jappa hat, the popular worn headgear for gentlemen of the day:
Under the fell clutch of circumstance
He had not winced nor cry aloud
Under the bludgeoning of chance
His head was bloody but unbowed.

"A heavy procession with the band of the Universal Negro Improvement Association headed the mighty throng from Orrett's pier along Port Royal Street, to King Street where a red carpet was befittingly laid and which stretched up King Street, covering the entire route of the procession to Liberty Hall, 76 King Street, where the procession halted and Garvey alighted to the thunderous and volcanic explosion of cheers and approbation from his people — his loving Jamaican people — one of the greatest people to be found anywhere in the world.

"Marcus gave an impassioned oration to the crowd within the precincts of Liberty Hall. The mighty orator that he was, he had his audience spell-bound, electrified and appreciative as some became moved and reacted with tears of compassion.

"That night at the Ward Theatre Marcus was given a rousing civic welcome under the Chairmanship of his Worship the Mayor, the Honorable Hubert Lasceive Simpson OBE, Mayor of the Corporate Area and member for Kingston in the Legislative Council of the day, Garvey's old pal and confidant of earlier times.

Previous page:
Mr Marcus Garvey welcomed on his arrival at the Pier. (left to right) Capt Shirley of Mr Garvey's personal body guard. Mr Garvey. Henrietta Davis.

King Street today the site where a red carpet was laid to welcome home the people's hero, Marcus Garvey.

Fittingly Garvey in replying to the welcome of the Mayor said:
'It matters not how straight the gate
How charged with punishment the scroll
I am the master of my fate-I am the
Captain of my Soul.' "The Ward Theatre rocked with the standing ovation of the overflowing throng."

Black people in Jamaica saw Garvey as their spokesman but the planters and merchants (the white/brown elite) necessarily saw him as an enemy. Anticipating his deportation, two years before, in 1925, the *Gleaner* had written "Whether Mr Garvey comes here shortly or five years hence there can be no doubt that he will prove a dangerous element in Jamaica unless it is made unmistakably clear at the very beginning that the authorities are not prepared to tolerate any nonsense on his part..."

Even earlier the *Gleaner*, in April 1924, had taken the view: "It is with profound regret that we view the arrival of Marcus Garvey in Jamaica. And it is with more than profound regret that we picture any leader of thought and culture in this island associating himself with a welcome given to him. But Kingston has reached such a level of degeneracy that there is no knowing what she will do.... A new spirit has passed over the lower classes which has nothing to commend it except its ignorance.."

The paper described Garvey's return as the "dumping upon us of a man who indeed is Jamaican but for whom the island as a whole, or the more intelligent section of it, has no use."

Rupert Lewis shows how the *Gleaner,* in frenzied paranoia, slandered Garvey and his organisation. He says: "Two of the main targets used were the Black Star Line enterprise for which Jamaican contributions had come, and Garvey's insistence on the paramount importance of African political emancipation. The *Gleaner* consistently propagandized against the financial contributions of Jamaicans and also said they already had a country. For them the idea of a 'great Negro Republic' was impossible and those who subscribed to it knew it was impossible."

BIG MEETING

AT
THE BAPTIST CHURCH, LUCEA.

—————

Wednesday Night, 19th, at 7 O'clock

Mr. Marcus Garvey, President of the Universal Negro Improvment Association of Jamaica will deliver an address on the aim and object of the Society.

A cordial invitation is extended to every citizen to attend. No one should be absent.

THE ASSOCIATION AIMS AT THE UPLIFTING OF THE PEOPLE OF JAMAICA.

It is supported by the most representative and educated of the Island.

Dont Fail to Hear Mr. Garvey. He is an Able Orator.

A SILVER COLLECTION AND DONATIONS TAKEN TO HELP THE WORK OF THE SOCIETY

ALL SHOULD ATTEND.

SANKEY HYMNS WILL BE SUNG.

God Save The King.

Despite these attacks Garvey never lost the support of the mass of the people, who acknowledged this in their large turnouts to his meetings.

Vivian Durham remembers poetically the early meetings after Garvey's return, and how people found his vision of 'success' for the black man irresistible. He says: "Whenever Garvey spoke it was electrifying. It was his silver-tongued oratory that inspired 11 million people to come into his organisation. It was Friday evening and the skies were overcast, the crowd were gasping at every word from his lips. As the poet said: 'Truth from his lips prevailed with double sway and fools who came to scoff remained to pray'. He ended his address by saying: 'They dragged me through the streets of Harlem like a common thief. But oh, thou God of Ethiopia, who when the Assyrians spat upon thee and Jews jeered thee, remember it was Simon of Cyrenica, the Negro, who helped bear your cross — can you forget the Negro now?' Tears ran down the cheeks of able-bodied men and hysteria befell young women of tender age.

"Garvey returned to a Jamaica where poverty wore rags and rascality wore robes. Where the tender and the loving ate crusts and the infamous sat at banquet. At a time when Jamaica was being ravaged by colonialism, there were no labour laws — if you asked for increased wage they would shoot the ring-leader. Terrible infant mortality — if you can think of Charles Dickens' England, where a man could go to prison for not working, when there was no work for him. Mentally the people were dumb, it was a sin to think, treason to pronounce new truth, and blasphemy to see yourself in any other capacity than a peon serf.

"The stripes of slavery were not yet healed and our only role when Garvey came was hewers of wood and carriers of water. Those were the conditions that drove Garvey to form the People's Political Party in 1929. He advocated a Polytechnic of Jamaica, minimum wage and a cultural training centre; these and other proposals became his undoing. The cry went up from the ruling elite 'the old dreamer cometh — let us kill him'.

"Garvey was a unique character, for in that sad period in history after the emergence of Hitler, and the ravishing of our race — the last race to come out of slavery, we thought it was the worst moment in our history. Garvey said no, 'Black people for hundreds of years were basking as a race in our own glorious civilization, when Hannibal crossed the Nile and Ethiopia gloried in her splendour, which has never been equalled by any civilization, while the white, European was drinking from the skulls of their ancestors. They were not civilized.' Garvey told the black people we had a civilisation but we lost it. Garvey soon found that the ambition of every black Jamaican in those days, a legacy inherited from British colonialism, was to be a white man. In those days our conception was that based on the rich man in his castle, the poor man at his gate. God made them high and lowly, each to their estate. There was a perversion of the Bible to suit the coloniser.

"Racially we had the mulatto class which encapsulated the relation of the slavemaster with his unwilling captive, the slave woman. They formed an ethnological problem, the slave child would go to school bare-footed. The child of the slave master would go to school in shoes and in a carriage, she was the idol of her black playmates — they would put her in a ring and sing: 'There is a brown girl in the ring tra-la-la-la-la, brown girl in the ring, tra-la-la-la-la, for she's just like sugar and plum'. This situation created a racial cleavage; it became the bastardisation of the Negro race. That slave-master child was always the enemy of the black; he was dastardly and cunning in his inhumanity to his fellow black neighbour. It was this class that bitterly resented Garvey, even to this day."

Opposite page:
At Garvey's meetings, people were struck by his oratory and the power of his message.

After Garvey returned, the British Colonial Government was not long in responding with repression. Garvey and his second wife, Amy Jacques, were denied visa entries to visit British Guiana or any of the British West Indian islands. In Trinidad there was an anti-Garvey lobby among some school-teachers, who in their journal were opposed to Garvey's visit. In Cuba, the Government banned the *Negro World* in 1928 and declared the UNIA an illegal organisation in 1929.

It was, therefore, very clear that the prime tactic of the colonial authorities was to isolate Garvey from the main body of his movement in the Caribbean, through a denial of civil and political liberties. Garvey, however, would still not withdraw from his international perspective and in 1928 he went to England. While in London he established contacts with African students and he spoke regularly at Hyde Park. At a public meeting at the Royal Albert Hall on June 6th, 1928, Garvey asserted the right to self-determination for all colonial peoples. He then toured Europe stopping in Geneva, where he presented a petition to the League of Nations on behalf of the Negro peoples of the world. It documented the world-wide economic exploitation and oppression of African people.

Garvey's activities in Europe were reported in the Jamaican press and pamphlets of his major speeches were published and distributed through the UNIA on his return. Garvey's strategy was to fight the limitations placed on him by the colonial authorities by making his activities international.

Garvey's re-entry into Jamaican politics came in 1928 when he formed the People's Political Party (PPP). Soon after Garvey held a meeting at the Ward Theatre, Kingston "to expose the *Gleaner*". Garvey declared: "I want everbody in Jamaica to understand that we are going to have decency in the political life of this country. The *Gleaner* has had its day. We are not going to have any more government by the *Gleaner*, we are going to have government by the people."

Garvey had thrown down the gauntlet and all the rich elite forces of Jamaica rose to the surface to challenge. Garvey's difficulties began in the course of his campaigning for legislative office in the Jamaican general elections due to take place in January 1930. The problem came when he issued his manifesto. Rupert Lewis describes it as an historical development for Jamaica and colonial society. He said: "Garvey's historic 1929 manifesto was the first practical and realistic anti-imperialist political programme in this country (Jamaica). It summed up briefly the major economic, political, legal and educational demands of the working people as a whole. It was on that basis that Garvey waged a campaign against imperialism and the big landowners." Garvey himself suggested that others should stand for election, but on certain terms. He said: "I recommend that the poorer classes of Jamaica — the working class — get together and form themselves into unions and organizations, and elect their members for the Legislative Council. With few exceptions the men in the Council are representing themselves and their class. The workers of Jamaica should elect their own representatives, and if the Government here will not pay the Legislators, as is done in England, and America, then the Unions and Organizations should pay these men so that they can talk out without caring whom they offend."

His manifesto became like a red rag to a bull; the programme was wide, ranging from economic reform, which included a minimum wage and an eight hour day, to land reform and a law to compel employment of not less than 60 per cent of the labour force. There were objections to a corrupt judiciary and he pointed out the need for legal aid. While on the education side he recommended the founding of a Jamaican university or polytechnic, the establishment of a government high school in the capital town of each parish for the supply of free education, and a parish library in the capital town of each parish. These were just a few of the many points on his manifesto. The Achilles heel, however, came with the tenth plank of the document — this declared that it would be his intention, if elected, to introduce the following law: "To impeach and imprison such judges, who in defiance of British justice and constitutional rights, will enter into illicit agreement with lawyers and others to deprive other subjects of the realm of their rights in such courts of law over which they shall preside, forcing the innocent parties to incur an additional cost of appeal, and other legal expenses, which would not have been but for the injustice occasioned by the arrangement of such judges with their friends."

In other words (to use the Jamaican colloquialism) 'The judge dem a mek case from dem verandah.' Garvey was promptly hauled before the Supreme Court of Jamaica on a contempt of court charge and was fined and sentenced to three months imprisonment. Garvey served his time in Spanish Town prison and was released on December 10th, 1929. The time he spent there has long since passed into popular legend as in this song by Culture.

Norman Manley, the architect of Jamaican independence (father of Michael), was not the prosecuting barrister in this case but did clash with Garvey in a libel case brought by a lady in relation to an article in his weekly paper. Manley says of the case: "He defended himself and did much to enhance his own reputation. He made a brilliant closing address to a Special Jury hearing the case. He was witty and amusing, took every advantage open to a litigant who defends himself and though I won the case, which was really quite indefensible, he got that jury to award the lady a bare half the damages we had expected to win. It was a fine performance."

Two Sevens Clash — Joseph Hill and Culture (1976)

What a lick and bambaya when the two sevens clash,
What a lick and bambaya when the two sevens clash,
My little ol' prophet Marcus Garvey prophesy say St Jago De La
Vego and Kingston is gonna meet,
And I can see with my own eyes, it's only a housing scheme that divides....
(Chorus)
Sometimes I ride to town on the overland and ground and sometimes
I ride to town on bus S82, say what
Look at the cotton tree down by the riverside and think of how beautiful it used to be,
Now it has been destroyed by lightning, earthquake and thunder I say,
say what
(Chorus)
They took Marcus Garvey down to Spanish Town police station,
And just as they were about to take him out,
He said: "As I pass through these gates not another prisoner shall pass before my words come true,"
And to this day — it remains the gate has never opened, say what
(Chorus)

Norman Manley prosecutes Garvey in a libel case but admires his wit and intelligence.

H. G. Delisser (1878–1944) Editor, the 'Gleaner' 1904–1942 and Secretary of the Jamaican Imperial Association. His paper hounded Garvey without mercy.

Sir Edward Stubbs, Governor of Jamaica 1926–1932. He was the man in charge when Garvey was deported from America.

On his release from prison, Garvey was at a severe disadvantage in respect of the forthcoming general election, little more than a month away. When the votes were counted and the figures announced Garvey was beaten by a massive majority and so were the other candidates he had actively campaigned for.

Partly due to his own bad judgement and partly due to the limited political franchise which was based on property qualifications (with only 7.75 per cent of the population registered to vote), Garvey's hopes for attaining national political honours in his native Jamaica were dashed, and the threatened disruption of colonial rule, which local officials feared his victory would have brought, was averted. Garvey had to fight on too many fronts; there was also the systematic character assassination by the *Gleaner*. Rupert Lewis points out that there were 121 articles which made reference to Garvey, either in editorials, letters to the editor, or news reports. Of these 121 items, 68 were unfavourable, while 21 were favourable and 32 neutral. Out of the total of 14 editorials, 12 were unfavourable, two were thought to be neutral. As if to dance on the grave of Garvey, the *Gleaner* then tells its readers why they thought Seymour Seymour, who beat Garvey in the election, was the right man for the job and of course it was nothing to do with the fact that he was brown. "The lesson to be learnt from the results of the election is patent: the vast influence which Mr Garvey was supposed to have exercised over the minds and actions of a majority of our people existed only in the imaginations of those who most dread his propaganda ... It was known that the wealthier households in the Plain of St Andrew would support Mr Seymour to the last man and woman, but some persons supposed that the peasant and the working classes would reply to the last man in support of Mr Garvey."

For Garvey, the basic power and influence of the UNIA could be seen to be crumbling. He had gambled on Jamaica as his strategic base from which to rebuild the movement. By 1930 he had lost and the UNIA was on the decline. Garvey sought England as his new base and, after his declared intention, the Colonial Secretary in Jamaica wrote to Military Intelligence in London with the following account of Garvey's defeat in Jamaica: "In the course of the summer (1930) it became my duty as officer administering the Government (in the absence of the Governor), for reasons into which I need not enter now, to dissolve the Kingston and St Andrew Corporation — a step which was inevitable and generally recognised as such. But you will readily imagine Marcus Garvey, already disgruntled and seeing his public life ending, displaying an intense hatred of me and of everybody concerned. His paper *The Blackman* contained violent articles against me describing the 'death blow to democracy' and all the rest of it, comparing me to Nero (rather a compliment really!) and so on and so forth. But the dissolution was effected with some celerity and took the principal malefactors rather by surprise so that the articles fell flat even among his supporters.

"Marcus Garvey thus lost his chance of appearing in the public eye and is, I gather, now entirely discredited. *The Blackman* has ceased publication: he has given up his printing establishment; he is selling his headquarters and his private house near me and, I break to you gently my dear Colonel, he has announced that he's leaving these shores for England, almost immediately. I wish you joy of him! I will advise you by what steamer he is arriving. Whether he intends to 'raise' the fiery cross in England or on the Continent, I do not know and I do not suppose he knows himself."

The reply from London is worth quoting: "We will keep a look out for him on his arrival here ... There is one thing quite certain, and that is, he can do very little harm over here as his campaign in this country some years ago was a distinctly abortive one.!''

In 1935 Garvey's wife Amy Jacques said goodbye to him as he set sail for England. Amy Jacques in her memoirs reflects on the last time she saw Garvey in Jamaica. She writes: "Anticipating his leaving the island, Garvey agreed to an auction sale of all our furniture, by the man who held the bill of sale on them, who collated every penny in reduction of the mortgage. The day after the auctioneer had ceased to cry going, going, gone, we stood in an empty house, except for a bedroom suite, the books and two large pictures and vases left unsold. This did not affect him as I thought it would. He looked forward to living in England despite his asthma and the damp climate; he would be at the hub of world affairs. He never felt crushed by crises; future events could overcome them, his view was not shortsighted. Two days later he left us for England, with instructions for me to rent out the home, get two rooms somewhere, as my mother's home was being remodelled and in time he would send for us .''

Amy Jacques Garvey, she later joined Garvey in England where they attempted to rebuild the movement.

Garvey, although brave about the possibilities in London, was still bitter at the dirty tricks that lost him the local election; in a moment of passion he wrote to the *Gleaner* (February 6th, 1930): "From my observation. . . .I am forced to conclude that Jamaica is indeed an ignorant community; it is limited in intelligence, narrow in its intellectual concepts, almost to the point where one can honestly say that the country is ridiculous . . . . ."

I don't think that Garvey is being contemptuous of Jamaica in the V.S. Naipaul mode, but rather speaking as a frustrated father to a son or as an older brother to a younger. This sentiment is important if we are to understand the real notion of a Jamaican hero; Garvey in this sense is a new kind of Jamaican hero — an anti-hero, who will stay on the outside until the nature of Jamaica has changed. In another place they would call it revolution. In Jamaica that revolution would have to deal head-on with the colour question. The difficulty in dealing squarely with this question was one of the most compelling reasons for Garvey's failure, in his lifetime, to make an impact politically in his home territory. But, nevertheless, his views are on the agenda of great Jamaicans and their movements in modern times, and is a reflection of the power and enduring quality of his thinking: from Bob Marley, who talked of the need for black people to emancipate themselves from mental slavery, to the People's National Party's (PNP) call for self-reliance, to the Jamaican Labour Party (JLP), who have claimed him as their hero of enterprise and private initiative. Nothing is new under the sun for Garvey and, as an anti-colonial champion, his ideas have laid the foundation of Jamaica's struggle for Nationhood.

The Jamaican Legacy

Garvey was well aware of the history of sexual exploitation in Jamaican slave society and how the female slaves were subject to rape and sadism by the white masters. Records tell how the white employees on the estate had a system of rotation where they would rape the most desirable females on the plantation over and over again.

The white people consisted not only of the planter's family but of men employed as overseers and managers. The general term for them was 'book-keepers', although in fact, they spent most of their time riding around the estate, seeing that the work was done. Housing was provided by the planter. It was obviously to the latter's advantage to employ single men. These men then formed the group which were to sexually exploit the females of the estate. After the planter had taken his prize pickings, then the book-keeper could exercise his own choice.

One of the major reasons for excessive violence on the estate was jealousy. A white wife would discover her husband involved with a mulatto or black mistress; she would then exercise her revenge on the girl. The story of a Jamaican planter's flash of temper after his mulatto mistress became jealous of his flirtations with a young girl is told in 'Jamaica Plantership' by Benjamin M'Mahan, which was a factual account. M'Mahan said: "Adam Steel (the planter) was living in the fashion of the country, with a free woman of colour, named Miss Marshall. She owned a young brown slave girl, named Sarah, about fourteen or fifteen years of age, who was a great favourite of her mistress. Steel, it appeared, was constantly trying to seduce this poor creature. Miss Marshall became jealous, and vented her spleen upon the girl, and one day accused her of being impudent to her, which in her jealousy, she imputed to Steel's attentions to her, and at the same time threatened the girl that she would make Mr Steel give her a flogging. Steel overheard all this, and determined to revenge himself both on the girl and Miss Marshall. He called out, 'I'll take care of you two, I shall have no more quarrels about me.' He sent for the driver, John Taylor, and four able people; poor Sarah was dragged out to the terrace in front of the house; Steel took his chair out, and sat down, so that he might not be tired during the prolonged punishment he designed to inflict. The girl was stretched out, and her body laid bare. I shall never forget the sight, she was the most beautiful creature, the picture of symmetry; her skin like velvet, without a mark upon it — alas! So soon to be disfigured by the horrid lacerations of the whip. The punishment commenced at half-past four, and was not finished till six o'clock, during which time the driver had to stop three different times to put new lashes to his whip... Her appearance was awful — I thought she was dying I was sick at heart I could bear no more, so I went into the plantain walk to get out of sight and hearing of the murderous work. I had then counted upwards of 300 lashes..."

The mulatto class, ironically born, in some part at least, of rape and sadism, nevertheless had a degree of power vested within its members — the fact that Miss Marshall (a mulatto) owned Sarah is indicative of this. John Stewart, in his account of Jamaica and its inhabitants tells us: "The brown children of the more opulent of the whites are educated in the island, or sent to Great Britain for that purpose. Such as have received a liberal education and do not follow the immoral example around them, are for the most part well behaved, respectable people."

The strange sight of daughters of Europeans at the same school as their illegitimate relatives, revealed the power of the browns. A new class appeared in Jamaica, which attempted to create an equivalent lifestyle to those of the ruling whites. Stewart explains: ''The more important people of colour, shut out from the general society of the whites, form a separate society of themselves. They have their own amusements, their parties, their visiting and their balls. The latter are fully as gay and as expensive as those of the whites; and as the brown females are the chief planners and supporters of these, the young dissipated of the white men, their admirers, form a distinguished part of those meetings of pleasure.''

There was no question that the browns wanted to be thought of as white. They despised that part of them which was black. But they also suffered from the rejection of the whites, whom they were trying to imitate. Anthony Trollope confirms the rise of brown power in Jamaica, he writes in 1859: ''Both the white men and the black dislike their coloured neighbours. It is useless to deny that as a rule such is the case. The white men now, at this very day, dislike them more in Jamaica than they do in other parts of the West Indies, because they are constantly driven to meet them, and are more afraid of them.

''In Jamaica one does come in contact with coloured men. They are to be met at the Governor's table; they sit in the House of Assembly; they cannot be refused admission to state parties, or even to large assemblies; they have forced themselves forward, and must be recognized as being in the van (sic). Individuals (whites) decry them — will not have them within their doors — affect to despise them. But in effect the coloured men of Jamaica cannot be despised much longer.''

The whites had good reason to feel threatened. The Jamaica census of 1861 gave the total population as 441,264, of which the whites constituted 13,816, the coloured 81,065 and pure blacks 346,374. The blacks, although the majority, lacked the skills, education and growing finance of the aspirant brown people.

This issue is indeed more than skin-deep, because the colour issues and the place of the mulatto in Jamaican society is the key to understanding Jamaica.

In Jamaica's history certain flashpoints have brought to the fore a major underlying legacy of slavery and that is the problematic nature of the African presence in modern Jamaican life. This was exemplified by the behaviour of the crowd at The National Arena where, in September 1986, Lisa Mahfood was crowned Miss Jamaica (World) amid misguided missiles discharged by a dis-

Beautiful children: Mirror, mirror on the wall, who is the fairest of them all?

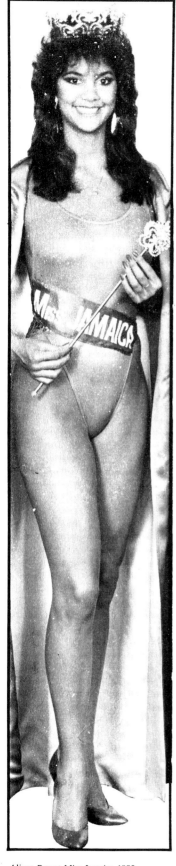

Alison Barnet Miss Jamaica 1985.

approving audience. Mahfood claimed fall Jamaican blood (her parents and grandparents are Jamaican, she reminds everyone) but is proudly described as being of "Arabian heritage". After the incident she enjoyed the passionate support of those Jamaicans rooting for her against the "nastyminded" and the "barbarians", as two *Gleaner* columnists described the rebellious crowd at the National Arena on the night of the crowning.

Professor Rex Nettleford commenting on the contest said: "There would be those who would insist that there is a built-in race and colour bias in the Miss World contest which helps not one iota with our own serious and more than skin-deep problems back here. The continuing marginalisation of the majority by strategies or institutional devices — whether economic, social, political or cultural — is neither wise nor just for this society."

The majority in this case refers to the bulk of the population which built Jamaica and also brought the society out of slavery. Nettleford again says: "If people from the so-called 'minority' groups can be shocked and disgusted by racist expressions against them, how much more shocked and irate must be the people from the majority who have been suffering racism in primary, secondary and tertiary forms for some 400 years."

Beauty contests and all other devices which serve to perpetuate this state of affairs have long proven divisive. The tune which the orchestra played to bring on stage half the contestants was — yes, the ring-game song: "There's a brown girl in the ring, Tra-la-la-la-la." We have long heard of brown-man governments, brown-man power, brown-man religion and brown-man culture being at the centre of life's ring-game with all others hopping, stepping and jumping around to the refrain, tra-la-la-la-la. A source of dissatisfaction and cause for alienation among many Jamaicans, it most certainly has been. That the tune with the words has been played more stridently in the recent past is a measure of how much this is brown-man's time. What is certain is that the refrain to "There's a brown girl in the ring" is not likely to remain a joyous "Tra-la-la-la-la" if those on the outside are required to stay perpetually out there merely to dance attendance.

Garvey's continual preoccupation with the danger of the mulatto did not arise out of a paranoia that most of his major opponents were of mixed race. (W.E.B. DuBois and in Jamaica, Seymour Seymour.) It arose from a desire to change the whole idea of what really constituted a Jamaican. In America the black man was not part of America — they had no rights and were seen as little more than serfs. In Jamaica, there was a greater sense of belonging but this was only achieved if the black man was prepared to "know his place" and deny Africa and worship everything white and brown.

The crucial issue was, who or what is a Jamaican? It was never satisfactorily resolved. Indeed, once the political battle for independence was over, the next question the new Jamaica asked itself was, who am I? With the Arawaks dead, who comprised the native population? A Jamaican was not an African, nor an Anglo-Saxon — it must be an expression of a mixture. For every 100 Jamaicans, 76.8 are of pure African descent, 0.8 pure European or white, 1.7 are East Indian, 0.6 are Chinese, with the remaining percentage being some combination of any of these.

As the pure white population has dwindled, historically the free coloureds became heir to the European position of power and regarded themselves as the rightful sons of the Jamaican soil since, of all groups in Jamaica, they were the ones that came directly out of the peculiar circumstances and conditions of early Jamaican society. After all, the argument seemed to go, the blacks can look to Africa, the whites to England, the Indians to India. But they (the mulattoes of mixed-race), must look to Jamaica. When someone says ''I am a Jamaican'' what they mean is that they are not African or Anglo-Saxon but a mixture. Jamaican politicians will never speak of Jamaica as an Afro-country. When going to speak abroad, they call on the national motto ''Out Of Many One People''. Jamaican society, post-independence, is a place where 'brown' becomes the ideal. This is not only in beauty contests but connotes membership of a privileged class — the majority black population live in abject poverty while brown equals wealth and power. The problem with relying on the mulatto as the solution to race differences, is that, if that is considered to be the norm, then the vast majority of pure blacks must be fringe or marginal.

Garvey had insight into this situation way back in 1911, but sadly even by the 1960s, when plans to make him into a National Hero were discussed, many had not understood or were not able to acknowledge the truth or importance of his message. A letter to the *Gleaner* at that time spoke for many: "Certainly, transporting of Negroes from America to Africa does not in the least affect the welfare of Jamaica. To my way of thinking we do not have in Jamaica any Negroes, Chinese, Syrians or English; we have Jamaicans and certainly if we are to spend thousands of pounds on a monument to honour someone, let it be spent to honour a Jamaican who has contributed tangibly to the development of the nation."

Even today, for all Garvey's legacy, one might say that attitudes among the black-skinned masses still exist which betray a self-contempt and a lack of self-confidence. Herein lies the greatest obstacle in the way of attempts to find an identity in terms of race. As Garvey argued — a people who do not believe in themselves cannot hope to have others believing in them. The symbolic poor peasant is indeed still glad to have her children rise above the peasantry, marry brown, and forget their roots.

Jamaican school girls, in a country still in search of its true nature.

Amy Bailey, a close friend of Marcus Garvey and a social worker during the 1930s and 1940s, recalled some of the entrenched racism of the time: "I began writing articles and when I went to 'Time Store' I remember meeting Mr Durie. He said to me 'Miss Bailey, I see you have been writing this thing but we don't discriminate you know, we have black girls.' So I looked around and I said, 'I don't see any of them here, Mr Durie.' He said, 'They are upstairs.' I said, 'Upstairs?' He said, 'Yes, they do the books upstairs.' I said 'You hide them away, up there.' I said, 'Mr Durie, when I come in here as a black woman, I want to see some of them down here. Otherwise it makes me feel that there is something wrong, that there is an inferiority complex about me and there is none.'"

****

However there was to be a group, movement and philosophy, owing its inspiration to Garvey and known as Rastafari, that would come out of the hills of the Jamaican countryside and arrive in Kingston. They looked on as everyone played the ring-game. They looked on in contempt and called the brown girl in the ring 'Babylon's daughter'. Since they were excluded from the game, from the brown-man's nativeness, they demanded repatriation back to Africa because Jamaica could never be their real home.

It is Garvey's legacy that provides the minds, men and ideas for the evolution of the Rastafarian movement. When Marcus Garvey left Jamaica for America, the UNIA at home fell into disorganisation, lacking any form of clear leadership. It became, however, the nurturing ground for the new radicals who were going to shake up Jamaica: among these were four Garveyites, Leonard Howell, Joseph Hibbert, Archibald Dunkley and Robert Hinds. In 1930 Ras Tafari was crowned King of Ethiopia. He took the name Haile Selassie to which he added "King of Kings", "Lord of Lords" and the "Lion of the Tribe of Judah", thus placing himself in the legendary dynasty begun by the Queen of Sheba and Solomon. For some of the Garveyites in Jamaica this came as a revelation. The God of Ethiopia, of whom Marcus Garvey had spoken, had appeared in the flesh, and all who needed redemption could now receive it from the most powerful ruler on earth before whom all kings had bowed. Black people throughout the world needed only to call on his name and the Lion of Judah would break all chains. They referred to him when Garvey said: "Therefore we must believe that the Psalmist had great hopes of this race of ours when he prophesied 'Princes shall come out of Egypt and Ethiopia shall stretch forth her hands unto God.'"

Opposite page:
Joseph N. Hibbert, early Rasta preacher.

Some saw this as evidence of Marcus Garvey as a true prophet, giving the prophesy of the coming of the redeemer who was going to deliver the black man from bondage, in much the same way as John The Baptist had prophesied the coming of Christ.

Leonard Howell, who was later to become the leading figure in the early development of the movement, began his ministry in the abject poverty of the West Kingston slums where he immediately developed a following. Hibbert began his mission in the outskirts of Kingston but later moved down into the ghetto where he found Howell expounding a similar doctrine to his own; Robert Hinds became Howell's deputy, with Archibald Dunkley, a Port Antonio seaman, the last to come to Kingston to complete the powerful quartet. From this point the movement gradually spread throughout the island, recruiting members from various splintered cells

Leonard P. Howell. Ex-UNIA member and founding father of the early Rastafarian movement. The authorities considered him insane or treacherous.

of old Garveyites. By 1934, under the leadership of Howell, Hibbert, Dunkley, and Hinds, a solid nucleus of Rastafarians had been established in Kingston.

Howell in 1940 founded 'Pinnacle' developing this important Rasta centre on an abandoned Sligoville estate. Situated a few miles from Spanish Town, Pinnacle was a retreat for the followers of Rastafari. It became their community, where the British colonial rule was defied, not by any direct action but by rejecting the law and government of Jamaica. Howell, as leader, was soon perceived as a threat to the established order and found himself sentenced to two years imprisonment for allegedly assaulting two local residents. It was at Pinnacle that the followers of Howell began to grow ganja and this also became an area of conflict between the community and the British colonial rule.

The coming of independence in 1962 only served to intensify the activist Rastafarian belief that Jamaican nationalism had no relevance to Rastafari. It remains central to the formal Rastafarian belief system that Ethiopia is home and that the brethren are strangers in Jamaica. One self-styled exponent of the Rastafarian doctrine, Bongo Dizzy put it this way: "Jamaica today is independent, yet English customs and laws and English instructions still lead us. The white queen still rules. The black Governor General is but her representative, how much voice do we have in saying what laws will pass at Gordon House? As far as I am concerned, politics was not the black man's lot but the white man's plot." In 1963 he wrote again saying: "The black man in this country and throughout the West has united with the heads of government in helping to build a better Jamaica, but we the black majority who have ploughed the soil, or planted the vineyard and gather the fruits thereof, we are not the benefactors. Those who benefit are the protectors. They share the crops, they boss the work and own the shares… the majority of Jamaicans are black why then are not the black supreme here? We want no promises we want fulfilment now. Three hundreds years of slavery in the Western world — what for? Jamaica's independence means a well without water, a treasury without money."

In October 1969, the radio and newspapers were full of the story of the visit of the Prime Minister and the leader of the opposition to Ethiopia and more importantly to Shashamene, where some 20 Rastafarians (including family units) began to settle. It seems strange to think of a government helping in the process of repatriating its own 'citizens' to another country. However, like the Thirties, the Sixties saw an upsurge in Rastafarian activity — much of this activity, however, was defensive, as Rastafarians came under terrible persecution from wider society by whom they were labelled a lunatic fringe, and from the police, who harassed them. The heaviest concentration of Rastafarians was to be found amongst the poor unemployed in West Kingston and their numbers could have been as high as 50,000.

The Government had ordered a team to investigate the Rastafari movement in 1960; it was the first serious study and was to become the basis for subsequent investigation and research. The report, amongst other things, suggested a Back To-Africa mission to investigate the possibilities of repatriation and on which Rastafarians should be represented. This was seen as a practical approach to one of the most central needs of the movement and it was at the same time making concrete a central plank of Garvey's dreams.

The visit by Haile Selassie to Jamaica in 1966 further pointed to the weakness of the concept of Jamaican nationalism. The authorities were forced once again, to reckon with the strength of Rastafari. The *Sunday Gleaner* reported: "Thousands of Jamaicans for whatever reason, were in a frenzy over an alien leader

New World African greets his past: Jamaican born Donald Leech greets members of a nomadic tribe who pass through Shashamene several times a year bringing salt from the Danakil region in the north by camel.

around whom they had woven legends. Perhaps for the first time many were seeing royalty embodied in the unaccustomed hues of Mother Africa, making it easy to establish kinship and identification.''

As Rex Nettleford says: ''In effect Selassie, a foreign head of state, was receiving from a sizeable segment of the Jamaican population, the unprecedented spontaneous enthusiasm that rightly belongs to Jamaican leaders who would normally be regarded as the embodiment of Jamaican nationalism.''

In 1964 historian C.L.R. James echoed a similar sentiment: "The Rastafari, the sect of Jamaican negroes who reject the bastardised version of British society which official and educated Jamaica seeks to foist upon them. They have created for themselves a new world, in which the Emperor of Ethiopia, Haile Selassie, is God on earth. His kingdom in Africa is the promised Heaven to which all the Rastafari elect will go, not when they die but when they can raise the money for the passage.''

Garveyism, therefore, informs the Rastafarian philosophy on two levels. First is his explicit statement that the black man should see God as black and second is, of course, the reference to Ethiopia and the emphasis on 'Back-To-Africa' which the Rastafarians see as mass repatriation. On both issues, however, the Rastafarians have interpreted Garvey in a way which is slightly oblique to his original meaning. Garvey essentially used a Christian frame of reference and certainly did not see Haile Selassie as God, in fact, during the Italian invasion by Mussolini, Garvey chastises the Emperor for leaving his country at a time of war, even though Haile Selassie had fled to England to seek assistance from the Foreign Office.

The attitude that Garvey took towards Haile Selassie after he arrived in England from Ethiopia was deeply criticised by both his friends and foes alike. In October 1935, he had argued that the Italo-Ethiopian conflict was an example of a country badly prepared for war. He later said in his magazine, *The Blackman*: "Haile Selassie kept his country unprepared for modern civilization, whose policy was strictly aggressive. He resorted sentimentally to prayer and to feasting and fasting

Haile Selassie: Garvey chastised him for leaving his country during the Italian invasion and missing out on the opportunity of uniting the black world in an effort to beat the Italians.

not consistent with the policy that secures the existence of present-day freedom for peoples whilst other nations and rulers are building up armaments of the most destructive kind as the only means of securing peace… and protection. The results show that God had nothing to do with the campaign of Italy in Abyssinia, for on the one side we had the Pope of the Catholic Church blessing the crusade, and the other, the Coptic Church fasting and praying with confidence of victory… It is logical, therefore, that God did not take sides, but left the matter to be settled by the strongest human battalion.''

Garvey's sharp attack on Ethiopia's rather archaic world showed no desire to romanticise its traditions; Garvey wanted a modern powerful Ethiopia and stressed to the Emperor that he read the sign of the times, which spelt out a United Africa — an Africa with some clout in the world. He said: "If Haile Selassie had negotiated the proper relationship with the hundreds of millions of Negroes outside of Abyssinia in Africa, in South and Central America, in the United States of America, in Canada, the West Indies and Australia, he could have had an organization of men and women ready to do service, not only in the development of Abyssinia, as a great Negro nation, but on the spur of the moment to protect it from any foe." Garvey went on to criticise the Emperor for leaning on white advisers and for refusing to receive a black delegation that had been seeking an audience with him.

In regard to the Rastafarian creed of repatriation, one of the expressions often used to describe the UNIA was the 'Back to Africa Movement'. In fact Garvey was unhappy with this description – he had argued that the UNIA advocated the return of only those pioneers capable of making a contribution to the development of Africa. Jah Bones, leader of the Rasta Universal Zion in North London, explained that for him repatriation was not a crude 'upliftment' of black people in the Diaspora back to Africa. He said: "Repatriation is linked to the desire for pride and respect, to have the knowledge that we have a black homeland, like China and India. It will come when the negative forces of discrimination and hardship will come together with an irresistible desire for a place in the sun. These forces will come to make repatriation a must. Garvey was prepared to take a substantial amount of black people back to Africa. If he had got the land in Liberia — then thousands of people would have left the Caribbean and the Americas for Liberia. It means whosoever in the right time, will be able to go back.''

Jah Bones. He sees repatriation as part of the irresistible desire for a place in the sun.

Although this is a black church, there still lingers behind the image of a white Christ.

The theme of repatriation is taken up in the song by Fred Locks, 'Black Star Liner' (1975). Many Jamaicans can remember with pride Garvey's ship docking in Kingston Harbour. One old man said in the *Gleaner*: "Garvey was the greatest thing that happen to black man. I remember the day when his Black Star Line ship land at Beef Market pier. Me just step up and look around and see black men piloting ship. That ship mash up after a while but today I see more black men building ship." For Fred Locks, as for many Rastafarians, the Black Star Line is strongly associated with repatriation, symbolising and indeed embodying, the physical means. A movement back to Africa. Fred Locks' song has become one of the anthems of Rastafari.

Black Star Liner — Fred Locks 1975

Seven miles of Black Star Liners coming in the harbour,
Seven miles of Black Star Liners coming in the harbour,
You can hear the people praying,
The elders are saying, that this is the time for which we've been waiting...
Seven miles of Black Star Liners coming in the harbour,
Seven miles of Black Star Liners coming in the harbour.
Marcus Garvey told us, freedom is a must...
that seven miles of Black Star Liners
would be coming one day for us...
Seven miles of Black Star Liners coming in the harbour,
Seven miles of Black Star Liners coming in the harbour,
Coming, coming, coming for I and I
For I and I, I can see the children running,
I can hear elders singing...
Freedom is a must....

Fred Locks sings the Rasta Anthem 'Black Star Liner'.

Party time in Shashamene:
Provides an opportunity for two Jamaican women (left) to invite their Ethiopian neighbours round for a feast.

The Black Star Line ships may have failed, but the urge to return to Africa remained. And others found different means of getting there.

The first West Indians to settle in Shashamene were Mr and Mrs Piper from Montserrat. They were fully assimilated into the community around Shashamene but to members of the Jamaican Mission they admitted their wish to see early settlement of the remainder of the land by Jamaicans and other West Indians, who wanted to live in Ethiopia. Haile Selassie is reported to have handed over the Shashamene land to the Pipers in the mid-1950s. The Pipers were members of the Ethiopian World Federation set up in New York, on August 25th, 1937. The EWF acted as a clearing house for financial and other contributions to the resistance to the Italian invasion of Ethiopia. Many were Harlem members of the UNIA who saw in Haile Selassie (or his American emissary Malaku E. Bayen) a new leader to fill the vacuum created by Garvey's deportation from America. This was particularly evident at rallies, when Bayen would refer to his audiences as "Fellow Ethiopians" and implore black Americans to "think Black, act Black, and be Black."

According to writer Claude McKay, Garvey's denunciation did not alter the general opinion towards Haile Selassie among American blacks. "To the emotional masses of the American Negro church, the Ethiopia of today (1940) is the wonderful Ethiopia of the Bible. In a religious sense it is far more real to them than the West African lands, from which it is assumed that most of the ancestors of Afro-Americans came. They were happy that the Emperor had escaped (from Addis Ababa) alive. As an ex-ruler he remained a symbol of authority over the Negro state of their imagination." This was also true for the Rastafarians in Jamaica — the EWF was committed to building a city in Shashamene. The movement had become international by 1940 with 22 branches in N. America, Latin America and the West Indies and with a membership said to be in the thousands and, in time, some pioneer settlers made their way to Ethiopia.

Many Rastafarians, however, have realised that the process of Africanisation can happen in Jamaica. In fact, by just living the Rastafarian lifestyle, they indulged in a process of symbolic repatriation — by changing Jamaica. In a parallel process, Jamaica has accommodated aspects of Rastafarian culture into the mainstream, nowhere more so, than in music. In fact, once Jamaican music had developed into a unique form — reggae — then the music of Rastafari, along with portions of its ideology, were embraced by the majority. And so it became the national music, adding strongly to the nativeness of Jamaica. Rastafarian, the Hon Bob Marley was, of course, a powerful exponent of this art. The lyrics of 'Africa Unite' echo the essence of Garveyite thinking.

Africa Unite — Bob Marley 1979

(*Chorus*)
Africans Unite, Afri-Africans Unite, yeh, Africans Unite,
'Cause we're moving right out of Babylon and we're grooving to our Father's land.
Behold how good and pleasant it would be, before God and man
To see the unification of all Africans,
As it's been said already, let it be done,
We are the children of the Higher man,
We are the children of the Rasta man,
United for the benefit of your people, unite 'cause it's later than you think,
Unite both abroad and at home, unite 'cause it's later than you think.

****

Bob Marley singing of the unification of all Africans.

In 1953 Pinnacle was back in operation, it was only then that the male members began to grow their hair in locks. They were called 'Locksmen', now known as 'Dreadlocks' or 'Nattydread'. It was said that, Howell ran 'Pinnacle' on the pattern of the Maroon communities of Jamaica. In the early days, followers numbered about 600. However by the time the authorities gave Pinnacle its final blow, in 1954, the Rastafarian movement itself was unstoppable and growing. In March 1958, a convention was held at Kingston which attracted 3,000 people.

For an old UNIA member like Howell, Rastafari as a movement was radically different. Jah Bones, who as a child in Jamaica saw the rise of one movement and the demise of another, explains the difference: "Essentially Garvey was a Christian. I don't think that he would share the Rasta notion that Haile Selassie is God in this time. Rasta is a cultural force, it is a religion, a spiritual movement. The UNIA members had a membership card and they paid subscriptions. Rasta is not an address, or number or even moral support. It is a total lifestyle, which determines what we eat, what we say and how we behave. The UNIA never really went deeply into the spiritual area – that was taken for granted. Marcus Garvey felt that as long as people went to church that was fine by him. Whereas the Rasta says you can't take the spiritual properties of life for granted because this is our livity. Garvey bequeathed us the opportunity of looking into life with spiritual eyes."

The cover of the membership cards of Howell's Ethiopian Salvation Union.

Ex-reggae singer Peter Tosh, who in September 1987, was assassinated in his Kingston home by gunmen, spoke before his death about the influence of Marcus Garvey. Tosh saw Africa as a source of power and inspiration. Africa for Tosh had a spiritual dimension which went beyond time and space. He said: "Before I was brought here, I was living a life profound. Flowers bloomed and waters flowed; the air was fresh, unpolluted; the skies were blue and the moon was yellow with stars uncountable. I remember when I use to live this life. Birds use to sing — I remember when I didn't have electronic music — when many birds came to sing, no technology could have recorded that harmony. Only in nature's way can those melodies be played again." He goes on: "My duty as a defender of the universe is to see to it, that all who stand to oppose light and love, and all that is constructive to keep life in function — my duty is to eliminate them — through the powers of the most high. He put me here to be a defender of the whole universe." Here Tosh romantically mixes a blend of Garvey and Rasta; had not Garvey, many years previously, described the function of men and women as being "The Lord of Creation" and not a slave?

Tosh felt that black people were still under the influence of slavery, but the teachings of Garvey gave these people the dignity to fight for a better world. Tosh said: "If Marcus Garvey was here now they would run him out of Jamaica and shoot after him the same way. . . . It's hypocrisy calling him a national hero. Garvey teaches my people to love themselves and be proud if you are black. Me proud this (pointing to his arm) one million times. He goes on: "This is brown government or a white government, it is not a black government, come to teach black dignity. The teaching of black dignity is subversive in a slave society. If a brown man and a black man go look work and the brown man can't read and the black man has advanced level — remember it's the brown man who is going to get the job — unqualified. We have no power to keep any man up there especially we who call ourselves Rastas — that is for the people who make 'Xs' and get vexes, right now I'll never vote, but when the government of righteousness comes, no man will vote for any man. It will be the voice of the people, that will be the voice of Jah."

Opposite page:

Playing together! A Jamaican and a Dominican compete in sport. Garvey was an inspiration for Caribbean unity.

Garvey would probably only agree with half of what Tosh was saying, he would feel that even when the system is bad we must use our vote and partake in a democracy. We must remember how hard Garvey found it to be elected to the Legislative Council and this was because the majority black population were disenfranchised. Garvey, would have similarly disagreed with Tosh's notion of power. Tosh said: "What is power? Is power to have money, to kill a man, to have nuff gal or go to school and get some Columbus Knowledge? Power is to cry Rastafari and you feel the earth shake and lightning flash. To call upon Jah and someone gets healed." Garvey would say that if black people are going to progress in the modern world, then they need some of that Columbus Knowledge but do not forget who built the pyramids.

Peter Tosh: He says that Garvey teaches black people to be proud of themselves one million times.

African — Peter Tosh 1975

Think of where you come from as long as you're a black man, you're an African
Check out your integrity you have the identity of an African,
If your complexion high, if your complexion low, if your complexion in between, you're an African.
Think of where you come from as long as you're a black man, you're an African,
Don't mind denomination that is only segregation, you're an African
Said if you come from Brooklyn, if you come from Manhattan, if you come from London you're an African,
If you come from Trinidad, if you come from Montserrat, if you come from Guyana you're an African.

Apart from reggae music, perhaps the strongest ambassador of African expression in Jamaica has been the National Dance Theatre Company, led by Professor Rex Nettleford. The spirit of Africa is reflected in many of the roles he chose to play as a dancer — roles which emphasise the African ancestral mode of expression: an obeah man in 'Myal', a shepherd in 'Pocomania' and a king in 'Kumina'. In 1987, as a tribute to the Garvey centenary, he choreographed 'Children of Mosiah', a vibrant work exploring the Garvey influence. In 1962, the National Dance theatre of Jamaica was launched — the same year as independence — and was given the blessing of the Jamaican government. Since then it has built up a varied repertoire exploring a combination of African dance, dances based on Jamaican Caribbean folk and ritual dance. Nettleford sees the company as an important standard bearer of independence and ancestral pride in the wake of the inculcation of metropolitan madness. He says: "As far as dance itself is concerned, it is a paradox that the circumstances of colonial history dictate that a dancing-people, as the majority of the Caribbean peoples undoubtedly are, must get approbation and critical affirmation from a non-dancing metropolitan country like Great Britain to convince themselves that they can achieve excellence in an art native to them." He goes on "But this is a second-order problem soluble in terms of the Jamaicans' willingness to liberate the dance from the 'minstrelsy syndrome' to which it deteriorated on the Plantation and restore it to its place of primordial necessity as ancestral Africa, like ancestral Man, knows it."

Dancers of the National Dance Theatre of Jamaica assert their ancestry.

Mutabaruka utters words of freedom in the spirit of Garvey.

Weh Mi Belang? — Mutabaruka

negro
nigga
West indian?
den a which country I belang?
chinese–China
indian–India
european-Europe
negro?
nigga?
West indian?
den a which country i belang
negro black
but negroland no
nigga–stupid
but stupidland no
west yes
but i nuh indian
den a which country i belang?

Another artist of Garveyite utterance is Mutabaruka. His Dub poetry, like Bob Marley's lyrics, looks at the particular Jamaican environment of poverty, self-hatred, violence, love and great pride — this strange and potent mixture — and then he projects on to an international level words of redemption for black people everywhere.

Mutabaruka attempts to preserve and assert the African in the 'Jamaican' — he clearly understands that during slavery, and after emancipation, the African presence was very much alive and was a major factor in shaping the life and culture of both black and white. In the poem we are given a Garveyite theme as the poet acknowledges the continental base of other people around him but is aware that somehow when he tries to discover his base there is a problem — instead he hears a quiet voice, telling him to forget Africa: "you're a Jamaican, an American, an Englishman . . . ."

Away from the religious and mystical world, Garvey's influence has also been felt in the development of secular politics in the Caribbean. Walter Rodney for instance, was an intellectual who revered the teachings of Garvey and developed them for his own analysis of the Caribbean and Africa. Rodney, who was from Guyana, was regarded as having one of the best minds in the Caribbean, and taught within the History Department of the University of the West Indies, the Mona campus, Jamaica.

While absent from Jamaica, attending a conference in Toronto, the Government took the opportunity to ban Rodney from re-entering the country — he had been in his post as a lecturer for less than a year.

The banning order was issued by Hugh Shearer, who was Prime Minister and, in fact, was the island's first black leader. At the news of the banning, serious rioting and demonstrations broke out on the campus and also in downtown Kingston, where 50 buses were burned out — 14 major fires were started in different parts of the city. Rodney was essentially Garveyite in his philosophy and he saw the critical importance of a Black Power movement in Jamaica.

In his book, 'The Groundings With My Brothers', Rodney explains what Black Power should mean in the West Indies. He says: "Black Power in the West Indies means three closely related things: 1. The break with imperialism which is historically white racist: 2. The assumption of power by the black masses in the islands: 3. The cultural reconstruction of the society in the image of the blacks.''

Rodney argues like Garvey for the brown man to realise that he is black and join his oppressed black brothers. It was when Rodney began to expose the hypocrisy of the Jamaican government on the notion of racial harmony that he became too hot to handle. He said: ''What we must object to is the current image of a multi-racial society living in harmony — that is a myth designed to justify the exploitation suffered by the blackest of our population, at the hands of the lighter-skinned groups.'' He goes on: ''The present Government (1968) knows that Jamaica is a black man's country. That is why Garvey has been made a national hero, for they are trying to deceive black people into thinking that the government is with them. The government of Jamaica recognises black power — it is afraid of the potential wrath of Jamaica's black and largely African population. It is that same fear which forced them to declare mourning when black men are murdered in Rhodesia, and when Martin Luther King was murdered in the USA. But the black people don't need to be told that Garvey is a national hero — they know that.''

Rodney describes the West Indies as historically ''the laboratory of racialism'' — he looks to the Rastafarians as representing the leading force of black consciousness in the area. He says: ''They have rejected this philistine white West Indian society. They have sought their cultural and spiritual roots in Ethiopia and Africa. So that whether there is a big flare up or not, there is always the constant activity of the black people who perceive that the system has nothing in it for them, except suppression and oppression.''

Walter Rodney the Guyanese historian who saw Garvey as one of the greatest influences on the twentieth century.

It was on the question of violence that the Jamaican government managed to secure a banning order on Rodney; the charge was that he had consorted with persons who had ''plots and plans to prepare a violent revolution in Jamaica.'' The Prime Minister, to back up his point, quoted from one of the speeches allegedly made by Rodney: ''Revolution must come. We must be prepared to see it through. We must stop talking and indulging in academic exercises and act. Who will be the first to come with me downtown and take up a machine gun?''

Garvey didn't discount the need for violence. He said: ''Any sane man, race or nation that desires freedom must first of all think in terms of blood.'' However, Garvey worked what some have termed a silent revolution, using the Black Star Line as a symbol of success to inspire the black man, who had always regarded himself as a failure.

The ban on Rodney was imposed because he was determined to expose the lie of the received notion of Jamaican nationalism. He said: ''The Government of Jamaica, which is Garvey's homeland has seen fit to ban me, a Guyanese, a black man, and an African. But this is not very surprising because, though the composition of that Government, of its Prime Minister, the head of state and several leading personalities, though that composition happens to be predominantly black, as the Brothers say at home, they are all white hearted.''

It is clearly to the Rastafarians that Rodney looks in encouraging Jamaicans to look outside that ring of despair and self-denial: ''you have to speak to Jamaican Rasta, and you have to listen to him, listen very carefully and then you will hear him tell you the word. And when you listen to him, and you can go back and read Muntu, an academic text, and you read about Nomo, an African concept for Word, and you say, Goodness the Rastas know this, they knew this before Jenheinz Jahn. You have to listen to them and you hear them talk about Cosmic Power and it rings a bell. I say, but I have read this somewhere, this is Africa. You have to listen to their drums to get the Message of the Cosmic Power.''

Hugh Shearer, former Prime Minister of Jamaica. He was instrumental in the banning of Walter Rodney from entering Jamaica.

Rodney was clearly strongly influenced by Garvey and his best known work, 'How Europe Underdeveloped Africa', is inspired by the Garvey vision of Africa, and the need to liberate it from colonial domination.

Rodney was a historian and as such had a clear understanding of Garvey's contribution to post-slavery black history. He said: "Marcus Garvey always preached the value of African history and culture. He wrote that 'For many years, white propagandists have been printing tons of literature to impress scattered Ethiopia, especially that portion within their civilisation, with the idea that Africa is a despised place, inhabited by savages and cannibals, where no civilised human being should go'. After dismissing that propaganda as completely false, Garvey continued: 'The power and the way we once held passed away, but now in the twentieth century we are about to see a return of it in the rebuilding of Africa; yes, a new civilisation, a new culture, shall spring up from among our people.'"

I remember when I was teaching English in a High School in London and I gave my class an exercise to stimulate their imaginations, I wrote "AFRICA" on the blackboard; they then had five minutes to write down as many words that came to them when confronted with this one word. I walked around to look at the words they had thought of — they had more or less produced the same list: Jungle, hot, flies, mudhuts, spears, savage, cannibals, naked, bananas and pigmy. I did the

A high school in Clarendon, Jamaica. Garvey maintained that a strong nation was built on self-pride; this would only happen when children learnt of the glory of their past.

same exercise when I was teaching in Jamaica and got a similar response to that of the English children.

Garvey's inspiration to Walter Rodney was to encourage him to counter this misconception of Africa, to demonstrate its rich and varied history, to show that Africa was the leader in science and the arts, while Europe was still passing through its so called Dark Ages.

The kingdom of ancient Ethiopia was Axsum where what is acknowledged to be one of the first written languages, Geèz, was in use. Ethiopian economic and cultural history dawns way before the birth of Christ at a time when Britain would have been classified as underdeveloped with little progression beyond a caveman society, awaiting the Romans to come and introduce roads and cities. The achievements of The Aksumite Empire can be seen to this day in the ruins of the cities, towns, reservoirs, dams and temples. Historians have also shown that Axsum was an international trading centre.

Walter Rodney uses Garvey to explain how white propaganda keeps many black people out of touch with this vital history, he says: "Ethiopians can differ in skin colour from light-brown to jet black, but none of them are really different from the black Africans outside Ethiopia. White propaganda likes to suggest that the achievements of Ethiopia are not the achievements of Africa. Marcus Garvey knew about this lying propaganda and made it look ridiculous. He wrote as follows: 'Inferior George Kersnor after describing the genius of the Ethiopians and their high culture during the period of 750 BC to AD 350 in middle Africa, declared the Ethiopians were not African Negroes. He described them as dark coloured races showing a mixture of black blood. Imagine a dark coloured man in middle Africa being anything else but a Negro. Some white men, whether they be professors or not, certainly have a wide range of imagination.'"

It has been this undermining of a serious black past that has been the most convincing point in the argument for the restitution of stolen black historical manuscripts

Niabinghi drummers in Jamaica.

and relics plundered during colonialism. The most serious of these plunders occurred in Ethiopia in 1867, when basically the whole of her recorded history was shipped to Britain and has never been returned to this day.

Rodney points to the inspiration which stems from possessing that certain knowledge that black people have a history that is long, interesting and vital — an inspiration from which a new Jamaica can be created. This is an understanding he sees that the Rastafarians already possess: "You know that some of the best painters and writers are coming out of the Rastafari environment. The black people in the West Indies have produced all the culture that we have, whether it be steelband or folk music. Black bourgeoisie and white people in the West Indies have produced nothing! Black people who have suffered all these years create. That is amazing."

One of the glories of Africa: The Giant Sphinx of Chephren at Giza. This Egyptian colossus is about 240 feet in length and 60 feet high. When Napoleon unearthed this great work, it was reported that he and his soldiers attempted to disfigure its black features by shooting at its face.

Marcus Garvey was no mere sterile political theoretician: he saw the fundamental importance of a cultural programme for the development of Jamaica and the black experience. Thus Garvey became one of the foundation stones for organised creative activity in Jamaica. An early centre of activity, Edelweiss Park, founded by Garvey, was located at 76 Slipe Pen Road in Crossroads, Kingston. Equipped with a good stage, dressing rooms, carefully designed acoustics, and a four-tiered amphitheatre, Rupert Lewis says of it: "Edelweiss Park became the most significant cultural-political centre for black people in the history of the island at a time when the arts were dominated by expatriates — both local residents and touring drama groups — and when a black face on stage was a curiosity."

One of the greatest contributions in the field of culture made by the Garvey movement in Jamaica was in the area of dance. As testimony to this fact a recently mounted exhibition by the School of Dance was entitled 'The Garvey Years'. The exhibition showed how Garvey had given these dancers their only outlet, whilst also providing a venue for ordinary people to go and dance (before night clubs and discos were fully developed).

The Edelweiss Park Amusement Company maintained a number of cultural units as professional groups on its payroll. Among these were the Follies, a group of dancers who ironically would dance in the French can-can style. The Follies also sang and acted and were trained by the director of entertainment, Gerdo Leon. Dancing took place every night to the music of quadrille players and bands specialising in the Susie - Q and other North American music styles. Garvey himself described the Park as a centre where people could relax and refresh themselves "after the heat and burden of the day."

Famous Jamaican dancer, Ranny Williams, started his career at the Park as a dancer before moving into drama: "I was first a hoofer (back line dancer). Soon I was a front line dancer and then a feature dancer with partners in front of the front line." The performers learnt all kinds of dances: the flip, the jitterbug, the charleston, swing and jazz. Dancer Kid Harold asserts that "the best professional dancers came out of the entertainment circuit provided by the Edelweiss Amusement Company. This is the main legacy of Garvey in this field."

Garvey also wrote and produced several plays. His 'Slavery-From Hut to Mansion' had a cast of 120 characters and was described as a "revelation of the horrors of slavery", mapping out the history of slavery, emancipation, and the struggles that followed.

His most elaborate play was 'The Coronation of an African King' which had scenes set in several African, European and West Indian capitals. It was an exposition of the UNIA's work and the attempts by Europeans and American governments to stem the tide of the Garvey movement. Garvey also wrote many poems: they were perhaps not great pieces but demonstrated, nevertheless, his interest in the arts as well as his versatility:

"Out of cold old Europe these white men came
From caves, dens and holes, without any fame,
Eating their dead's flesh and sucking their blood,
Relics of the Mediterranean flood;
Literature, science and art they stole,
After Africa had measured each pole,
Asia taught them what great learning was,
Now they frown upon what the Coolie does.''

The statue of Marcus Garvey stands outside the St Ann Parish Library.

Marcus Garvey also becomes an inspiring influence for modern Jamaican musicians both directly and indirectly through the Rastafarian philosophy. Edward Braithwaite says of Jamaican Music:
"Jamaica: fragment of bomb-blast, catastrophe of geological history (volcano, middle passage slavery, plantation, colony, neo-colony) has somehow miraculously — some say triumphantly — survived. How we did it is still a mystery and perhaps it should remain so. But at least we can say this : that the secret and expression of that survival lies glittering and vibrating in our music."

The greatest of these musicians was Bob Marley who came from the same parish as Marcus Garvey, St Ann. Garvey's philosophies affected Bob Marley profoundly:

So Much Things to Say — Bob Marley 1977

"They got so much things to say....
But I'll never forget, no way
They crucified Jesus Christ
I'll never forget, no way
They sold Marcus Garvey for rice....
So don't you forget no way
Who you are, where you stand in the struggle."

During the Sixties there was a surge of interest in Garvey's beliefs. By the mid-Sixties this interest coincided with the birth of a deeper questioning of Jamaican society. Journalist Steven Davis asked Marley, "Are you going to Africa someday?" Marley replied: "Yeah, mon! Time is now, y'know what I mean? Is plenty of I and I.

"Marcus Garvey seh: 'Africa towards Africans.' Ya kyaan argue with that. All that is causin' the problem is devil needin' everybody's life. But here ya kyaan work for what ya want. Ya can never reach the goal. The system kill people so we must kill the system. Every mon wan fe drive car, nobody wants to ride donkey. Only one government me love, the government of Rastafari. We come from Africa and none of the leaders want fe accept it. They want us fe think we all Jamaicans. The majority of people in Jamaica want fe go home to Africa, but the leaders say you must stay and die here. Today is not the day, but when it happen 144,000 of us go home. Politicians don't care fe people only Jah care. Seh, every man for himself, and God for us all. Yeah mon, This is war! Jamaica is hell y'know. Until we find our roots again politics will still be a thing. If we find the roots again, we can live."

Redemption Song — Bob Marley 1980

Old pirates, yes they rob I, took I on a slavers ship,
Minutes after, they took I from the bottomless pit,
But my hand was made strong by the hand of the Almighty,
We'll forward in this generation triumphantly.
(Chorus) Won't you help me sing, another song of freedom for all
I ever had.....
Redemption Song, redemption song.
Emancipate yourselves from mental slavery,
None but ourselves can free our minds,
Have no fear for atomic energy,
For none of that can stop the times,
How long shall they kill our prophets while we stand aside and look,
Some say that's just a part of it, we've got to fulfill the book
(Chorus and fade)

Bob Marley — true heir of Marcus Garvey telling black people to free themselves from mental slavery.

Burning Spear (Winston Rodney). He keeps the flame of Garvey going in songs that are rooted in his environment.

Another great musician from the Parish of St Ann, Winston Rodney, better known as 'Burning Spear' lives in St Ann's Bay, literally round the corner from where Garvey lived as a boy. Spear has been the most up front in drawing on the message of Marcus Garvey for his lyrics and inspiration:
"Marcus Garvey words come to pass, Marcus Garvey words come to pass, Can't get no food to eat, can't get no money to spend, woe woe woe.."

Burning Spear lives round the corner from where Garvey used to live.

After we managed to devour four mangoes Spear and I went into his makeshift practice room where he told me how the song came to him under Garvey's inspiration: "Right now," said Spear, "that song sums up the condition of the people, no proper food, education: it's prophecy. The second step in my Garvey journey," he went on to say, "was the song 'Follow Marcus Garvey's footstep'."

I put it to Spear that he seemed to be saying no one remembered Marcus Garvey ten years ago. Did he feel that it was only now (at the hundredth anniversary) that people are remembering Garvey? "Yes that's why I sang 'No One Remembers Garvey'. Many people recreate this remembrance for only a short-time by saying that they are going to celebrate his 100th anniversary and after they go on as if he never existed." He recalls that it was with a degree of trepidation that he began to cry out "Marcus Garvey" in his African call and response melody.

He says: "I felt much doubt in singing about Garvey at first. I felt that many people might not check for it and I thought I might be trying to sell something that people didn't want. Anyway I went down to the civic theatre in my town and got involved in a show. Come rehearsal I got up and start singing 'Marcus Garvey words come to pass' They say...'No man wha' ya deal wid we nuh want nuh turn like dem deh.'

"I said let me sing a different tune, so I sang: 'Do you remember the days of slavery'. Then one man said: 'Wha' ya chat bout man. We want something we know bout'. I said to him, 'don't you remember that it was me and you who went through it, with all those chains and shackles'. They never took my two songs but then I just left it....It wasn't until 1974 that I returned to the theme of Marcus Garvey, but this time I wasn't having any doubts I just sing 'Marcus Garvey words come to pass'."

We looked out at the small primary school which was near the site of Garvey's old school. The children appeared happy and carefree. But Spear reminded me of the harsh reality behind the smiles — the lack of books, furniture and the terrible overcrowding. He went on to say: "Out of this work I hope....to reach the stage, where it will become a school subject to learn of Marcus Garvey. You know I was sitting here when some vibes come to I man and me just sing:
'Now they are late, so late
They come running through the gate, This gate of Marcus Mosiah Garvey
One hundred Anniversary.
Now you are late man, very late so late.
Come running through the gate of Marcus Mosiah Garvey
One hundred Anniversary
You're late still late'."

Burning Spear nurtures the hope that Marcus Garvey will be truly remembered. It is partly for this reason that he has decided not to live in Jamaica's capital, Kingston: "In the...countryside of St Ann, with its hills and seafront, an artist can make a lot of connections with the environment. It gives me good vibes, it's a force. Bob Marley came from here and I know he got much inspiration from his home parish, Marcus Garvey the same."

Burning Spear is a great soccer player. Earlier I had watched him training on the beach, juggling his football as if it were attached to his foot with invisible elastic. He once said: "Rasta is like football — a man must learn to control his world, be skilful, have the right timing, he must know when to hold and when to let go. In order to control it, he must be fit — eat the right food and not pollute his body. To control the ball, you must have tactics and a plan, this you will know if you read and meditate upon the word of Jah.'' He agreed that that was how Garvey saw his task and in further concurrence with Garvey, he affirms that Africa must be one, before the black man can have any say in this world. ''Black people should hold each other, we have to be strong in these days.

"If the black man liked himself then a place like Africa would never be under so much problems. When the East has a problem the West say it's not my problem. The North is in trouble and the South say it's not may fault. If Africa has problems it's for the whole of Africa to see it as their problem. Man has to stand up. If all run that will make Africa weak."

The body of Marcus Garvey was returned to Jamaica in 1964, he was given a State funeral and made a National Hero. Sadly the body laid in the catacombs in London for over twenty years. The danger is to forget Marcus Garvey.

David Hinds of British reggae group Steel Pulse who sing of Garvey in all their albums.

Not King James Version — Steel Pulse 1985

A dis ya version
A no King James version
'Cause out of Africa
Came the Garden of Eden

Hidden from me I was never told
Ancient prophets black and bold
Like Daniel, King David and Abraham
Israel were all black men
I don't wanna lose you

Japhet tried his best to erase
The godly parts we played
I says he came and took
And never mention in his book...no

In Esau's chapter of history
So little mention of you and me
We rulers of Kingdoms and dynasties
Explored this Earth for centuries
I don't wanna lose ya
Phoenicians, Egyptians and the Moors
Built civilization, that's for sure

Creators of the alphabet
While the West illiterate, yeh

Slavery came and took its toll
In the name of John Bull Dog
Said we turned our backs on God
Lost the powers that we had
Now our backs against the wall
Ask ourselves about the fall
Rise rise rise
Hold on to your culture.

Rally Round — Steel Pulse 1982

Marcus say, Marcus say, red for the blood
    that flowed like a river
Marcus say, Marcus say, green for the land,
    Africa
Marcus say, Marcus say, yellow for the gold
    that they stole
Marcus say, Marcus say, black for the people
    they looted from......

Garvey spoke to the true nature of the Caribbean problem. After emancipation in 1838 there was the destruction, not only of the institution of slavery, but of the total society itself. The Caribbean was the only totally slave society known in history, where the entire population was slave to most absent owners. This meant that after emancipation, power descended to those who did not have time to form into groups with a common aim. It is remarkable that a country like Jamaica managed to create groupings of power rather than violently explode. Emancipation did, however, leave the black mass without any access to any institutions of power that remained, that is, Legislative Council. It left them dangerously isolated from power. The black mass were in a country they neither controlled nor felt part of at a time when the world was developing rapidly. It is in relation to this problem that we find the real genius of Marcus Garvey. He saw that a society like Jamaica, with its isolated black mass, would be overwhelmed by developed countries if it did not change its nature. Garvey says: "You have your own King, your own emperor, your own pope, your own dukes, your own everything — therefore don't bow down to other races for recognition. Don't allow the other nations to get ahead of you in anything, follow the idea of the Japanese — every ship the other races build, the Japanese build one, every university the other races build for teaching men, the Japanese build one. Do the same. Always have your own because there will not be enough accommodation for you later on. Create your own."

It is this issue that has never been seriously tackled by any political figure since emancipation. Precisely because West Indian society was unique before and, indeed, after slavery, there are no models for the creative use of individual energy. Most attempts have missed the boat. There is a need for a proper model — not of reconstruction, because there is nothing to reconstruct — the only thing to be done with a total slave society is to abolish it. There is a great difference between West Indian and North American slavery. The abolition of the latter led to a reform of that society while in the Caribbean, slavery could never be reformed. The society was abolished and there was a need to build institutions from scratch. The black people of North America had no option but to join a society that continued — they could only assert themselves within the structure of the society in which they lived.

Garvey was saying to the Caribbean to join the world, and to do so from a position of strength, in self-knowledge and race pride: "The difference between the strong and weak races" he says, "is that strong races seem to know themselves; seem to discover themselves; seem to realize and know fully that there is but a link between them and the Creator; that above them there is no other but God and anything that bears human form is but their equal in standing and to that form they should bear no obeisance; there should be no regard for superiority. Because of that feeling they have been able to hold their own in this world; they have been able to take care of the situation as it confronts them in nature; but because of our lack of faith and confidence in ourselves we have caused others created in like image to ourselves, to take advantage of us for hundreds of years."

Garvey also understood and perhaps he was prophetic in this, that in order to remedy the post-emancipation problem, in terms of power and isolated individuals, those individuals, the majority of whom were black, must by definition, be in control of their own institutions. Garvey also sought ways of effectively dealing with creative individual energy. He knew that if this was not tackled those individuals would be alienated from power and then they would attempt to take power for themselves, resulting in a fractured and even barbaric society.

Jamaican mixed cane cutting gang around 1890 (nearly 50 years after emancipation), almost as driven, enduring and anonymous as actual slaves.

Garvey gave millions of Caribbean people a sense of pride in particular, race pride, and so enabling them to take their place in the world. He says proudly: "Never allow anyone to convince you of inferiority as a man. Rise in your dignity to justify all that is noble in your manhood (womanhood) as a race:

"My race is mine and I belong to it.
It climbs with me and I shall climb with it,
My pride is mine and I shall surely honour it,
It is the height on which I daily sit."

The Price of Peace — Jimmy Cliff

"You stole my history
Destroyed my culture
cut out my tongue
So I can't communicate
Then you mediate
And separate
Hide my whole way of life
So myself I should hate...."

Opposite page:
Jimmy Cliff a poet for all times, sings of the struggle against self-denial.

Black girl in the ring, Miss Jamaica (Universe) 1987, Janice Sewell.

Garvey would have loved this song by Jimmy Cliff which touches the essence of the inner anguish which is the Jamaican Caribbean reality.

A victor of this struggle was Miss Jamaica Universe winner for 1987, Janice Sewell, who was one of the first dark-skinned entrants to win the competition and acknowledged the importance of Garvey in her thinking: "I did not know much about Garvey until later in my life when I started reading on my own about the UNIA and so on. It is important for black people to come together and realise their potential and become more conscious because we have as much ability and talent as any other race."

When it comes to Caribbean unity, this 'consciousness' has often been forced to take a back seat to separate interest, this also faced the UNIA during Garvey's time. The West Indies is but precariously held together by the University of the West Indies, Calypso, reggae, Rastafarians and cricket. There is also the problem of foreign domination, as Professor Rex Nettleford has said. "So the Colonial Office saw us (and we accepted it ourselves) as the British West Indies, while today the United States Administration has conveniently scooped us up into a Basin. Colonial governors could ban the *Negro World* and deport troublesome Garveyites from island shores. Today the battle for the region's minds is via satellites, theatrical evangelism, and scholarships to US places of learning."

Although Garvey is a Jamaican Hero, he would not be bound by petty nationalisms but saw Jamaica as part of a vibrant black world, united in the same source which is Africa. His legacy for the Caribbean is an agenda for independence, where what is created at home is not regarded as inferior to the 'Masters' of America, Europe or Japan. Garvey made sure he travelled all of the West Indies, attacking the petty divisions that divided the islands. In a speech delivered at the Ward Theatre, Kingston on Sunday December 18th, 1927 he said: "You all know how the different West Indians despise each other, how the Jamaican despises the Barbadian and the Barbadian despises the Jamaican and all the other islanders hate each other to the point where in America, they would not assimilate. They worked against each other and the American Negroes worked against them and they were all pulling against each other. The Universal Negro Improvement Association was founded in 1914 after my experience of travel in South America, in Central America, in all the West Indian islands and in Europe, seeing well the need for greater unity amongst the Black people of the world." He goes on: "Therefore the American Negroes and the West Indian Negroes are one, and they are relics of the great African race which brought into the Western world and kept here for 300 years. I told them in Harlem that it is my duty to reunite the Negroes of the Western world with the Negroes of Africa, to make a great nation of black men (applause)."

Although dead Garvey has left one of the richest legacies in memory.

Kwame Ture admits that Garvey was a great influence when he first developed the concept of black power.

C.L.R. James sees Garvey as the man that gave black people hope by changing how they should view history.

Rastafarians see Garvey as a prophet.

Conclusion

It has been said to me on a number of occasions by old Jamaican UNIA members that it was only when Martin Luther King visited Jamaica that he was really moved with a burning desire for freedom and consequently became a real threat to the American authorities. King said during his 1965 visit; "in the light of the many unpleasant and humiliating experiences with which I have to live, I am glad to feel like somebody in Jamaica. I really feel like a human being."

He laid a wreath at Marcus Garvey's shrine and said: "Marcus Garvey was the first man of color in the history of the United States to lead and develop a mass movement. He was the first man, on a mass scale, and level, to give millions of Negroes a sense of dignity and destiny, and make the Negro feel that he was somebody.

"You gave Marcus Garvey to the United States of America, and he gave the millions of Negroes a sense of personhood, and a sense of manhood, and a sense of somebodiness.

"As we stand here let us pledge ourselves to continue the struggle in this same spirit of somebodiness...in the conviction that all God's children are significant...that God's black children are just as significant as his white children. And we will not stop until we have freedom in all its dimensions."

For King to feel a sense of freedom in Jamaica is not surprising, it's the same spirit that Garvey brought to broken black Americans after the First World War. In the hills of Jamaica, which rise above the brutality of the plantation and the colour madness of Kingston, a man or woman can look across the Altantic and see the great Ashanti tribes and the wonders of Axsum in Ethiopia. Garvey came to America, like a good Maroon, protected in the hills of St Ann, with a clear view of the continent that he had come from. Martin Luther King in his famous 'I Had A Dream' speech talked about climbing the mountain, this could have easily referred to his Jamaican experience. What turned on Martin Luther King as with all the other children of Garvey, was the simple but profound vision that the black man could be a success in the world.

Garvey did not preach racism, what he said was that in order for black and white to hold hands in the world, a black man's hands needed to be made strong. He saw that historically white hands had crushed the black man and made him a slave, raped black women and stolen black history and dignity. He then looked at his own time and pointed out the dangers for those who would take the communist or integrationist road, the white hands this time lead the black man like a child or a donkey, he must not reason why, but follow the party line.

What is interesting, is that the big black names of the twentieth century — DuBois, Padmore and C.L.R. James — make excursions into the white wilderness of communism and integrationist politics, but they all in the end have to come back to Garvey.

What Garvey achieved, was to undo the consequences of slavery — a black race drifting aimlessly, without dignity, history and a real place in the world — Garvey made the black experience universal, that is, he brought together black people in Africa, the Caribbean, South America, North America and said simply that this is one experience. That no matter where you are in the world if you are black you have a rich Continental base which is Africa.

Bibliography

Barrett, Leonard E., *The Rastafarians*, Heinemann, 1977
Bishton, Derek, *Blackheart Man*, Chatto and Windus, 1986
Blyden, Edward, *Black Spokesman*, Frank Cass, 1971

Cashmore, Ernest, *Rastaman*, George Allen and Unwin, 1982
Clarke, Johnson Henrik, with Amy Jacques Garvey, *Marcus Garvey and the Vision of Africa*, Random House, 1973
Clarke, Sebastian, *Jah Music*, Heinemann, 1981
Cleaver, Eldridge, *Soul On Ice*, Jonathan Cape, 1969
Cronon, E.D., *Black Moses*, University of Wisconsin Press, 1966
Cruse, Harold, *The Crisis of the Negro International*, New York Morrow, 1967

Davis, Stephen and Simon, Peter, *Reggae Bloodlines*, Heinemann, 1979
DuBois, W.E.B., *The Negro*, Oxford University Press, 1972

Edwards, Adolph, *Marcus Garvey, 1887–1940*, New Beacon
Essien-Udom, E.U., *Black Nationalism — A Search For An Identity in America*, University of Chicago Press, 1962

Fanon, Franz, *The Wretched of the Earth*, Penguin, 1974
_____ *Black Skin, White Mask*, Grove Press, 1967
Fryer, Peter, *Staying Power-The History of Black People in Britain*, Pluto Press, 1984

Garvey, Amy Jacques, *The Philosophy and Opinions of Marcus Garvey*, Atheneum, 1980
_____ *Garvey and Garveyism*, Collier Books, 1963

Henriques, Fernando, *Children of Caliban — Miscegenation*, Secker and Warburg, 1974
Henzell, Perry, *Power Game*, Ten. A Publications, Jamaica, 1982
Hill, Robert (ed), *The Marcus Garvey and UNIA Papers Vols 1,2,3,4,5*, University of California Press, 1983

James, C.L.R., *At The Rendezvous of Victory*, Allison and Busby, 1984

Kerr, Madeline, *Personality and Conflict in Jamaica*, Liverpool University Press, 1963

Leomone, Maurice, *Bitter Sugar*, Zed Books Ltd, 1985
Lewis, Rupert, *Marcus Garvey — Anti-colonial Champion*, Karia Press, 1987
Long, Edward, *The History of Jamaica 3 vols*, London, 1774

Maglangbayan, Shawna, *Garvey, Lumumba, Malcolm: Black Nationalist Separatists*, Third World Press, 1972

Mailer, Norman, *Cannibals and Christians*, Andre Deutsch, 1967

Mais, Roger, *Brother Man*, Heinemann, 1982

Malcolm X, *The Autobiography of Malcolm X*, Penguin, 1980

Manley, Michael, *Jamaica: Struggle in the Periphery*, Third World Media Limited, 1982

Martin, Tony, *Race First: The Ideological and Organizational Struggles of Marcus Garvey and the Universal Negro Improvement Association*,
_____ *Marcus Garvey, Hero*, The Majority Press, 1983
_____ *The Pan African Connection*, T.M. Press, 1983

M'Mahan, Benhamin, *Jamaica Plantership*, London, 1839
1982.
Morris, Ivor, *Obeah, Christ and Rastaman*, James Clarke, 1982

Mosley, Leonard, *Haile Selassie: The Conquering Lion*, Weidenfeld and Nicolson, 1964

Nembhard, L.S., *Trials and Triumphs of Marcus Garvey*, Jamaica Times Press, 1953
Nettleford, Rex. M., *Indentity Race and Protest in Jamaica*, William Morrow, 1972
_____ *Caribbean Cultural Identity: The Case of Jamaica*, Institute of Jamaica, 1978

Olisanwuche, Esedebe, *Pan Africanism*, Howard University Press, 1982

Owens, Joseph, *Dread-The Rastafarians of Jamaica*, Sangster's, 1976

Patterson, Orlando, *The Children of Sisyphus*, Longman Drumbeat, 1982
_____ *The Sociology of Slavery*, Sangster's, 1973

Plummer, John, *Movement of Jah People*, Press Gang, 1978

Post, Ken, *The Bible as Ideology: Ethiopianism in Jamaica 1930–38*, Allen and Johnson

Roberts, W Adolphe, *Six Great Jamaicans*, Pioneer Press, 1957

Rodney, Walter, *A History of the Upper Guinea Coast*, MR Press, 1970
_____ *How Europe Underdeveloped Africa*, Bogle L'Ouverture, 1972
_____ *The Groundings with my Brothers*, Bogle L'Ouverture, 1975

Schwab, Peter, *Haile Selassie 1, Ethiopia's Lion of Judah*, Nelson Hall, 1979

Stone, Carl, *Class, State and Democracy in Jamaica*, Blackett, 1985

Ullendorf, Edward, *Ethiopia and the Bible*, British Academy, 1967
_____ *the Ethiopians*, Oxford University Press, 1973

William, Chancellor, *The Destruction of Black Civilization*, Third World Press, 1976
Williams, Eric, *Capitalism and Slavery*, Andre Deutsch, 1981